How The Word Heals

How The Word Heals

◆

Hypnosis in Scriptures

Dr. John D. Lentz

For Chuck,
Your wisdom & knowledge
as found me for a young man
of your age. It was great
to talk with you. Thanks
for the insight.
John 12/15/03

Writers Club Press
San Jose New York Lincoln Shanghai

How The Word Heals
Hypnosis in Scriptures

Writers Club Press
an imprint of iUniverse, Inc.

For information address:
iUniverse, Inc.
5220 S. 16th St., Suite 200
Lincoln, NE 68512
www.iuniverse.com

ISBN: 0-595-21720-6

Printed in the United States of America

This book is dedicated to you,
if you let or have let the scriptures,
become healing to you.

2Timothy 3:16 All scripture is inspired by God and is useful for teaching, for reproof, for correction, and for training in righteousness, 17 so that everyone who belongs to God may be proficient, equipped for every good work.

Contents

Acknowledgements

I have a great debt to Jeff Zeig Ph.D. for his consultation, mentoring, encouragement and friendship. In addition to his invaluable intangible offerings he provided two tangible contributions. He suggested the Beatitudes be evaluated for their Hypnotic qualities and he generously offered his list entitled GIFT WRAPPING AND PROCESSING to be used as a basis for evaluating the hypnotic qualities of the scriptures. His ongoing friendship and encouragement have kept this project alive on a number of occasions. Dr. Zeig is known worldwide as one of the most prestigious advocates and promoters of Ericksonian Hypnosis and psychotherapy. People who know much about Hypnosis and therapy have encountered his work or influence, and are well aware of who he is. However, he is also one of the most gifted speakers and presenters anywhere. Sometimes the brilliance of his interventions go unnoticed by audiences because his ability makes what he does look so easy. On many occasions I have seen very sophisticated people coming away from his work feeling good and not really knowing how come. People who attend his workshops get more than they bargained for because he inserts so many positive seeds in the workshops that most recipients go home with positive assistance they didn't know was being offered. His style gave me the inspiration that since he did this routinely for people why shouldn't the Bible also be intentionally doing similar things.

I also owe more than could be easily listed to David Steere Ph.D. for his belief in me, and my work. His ongoing encouragement and especially his friendship, has been a constant source of support. The people who know me also know my fierce loyalty to and appreciation for David's expertise, mentoring, and his great skill as a therapist and teacher. David's careful reading and suggestions were invaluable. His contributions to my life and this work are enormous. I highly value his wisdom, deep commitment to God and especially his compassion and care for others. Seeing how skillfully, and in such gifted ways David repeatedly used words to bring healing to others, was always inspiring. Yet, even more inspiring was his genuine delight when people got free from dysfunction. His genuine delight showed me ways that God could also take similar delight.

Thanks also go to Anne Mason, Cyndi Hayslett, Betty Kassulke, Monty Hall, Teresa Lloyd, Sherry Steinbock, Jonathan Shippey, Sue O'Malley, Sandra S. McCauley, and Mike Rankin, Wayne Oates, Cameron Lawrence, Stacey Lentz, Seth Lentz, Abby Flint, and Debbie Lentz for their suggestions, encouragement, and support.

I owe a debt of gratitude to Kay Stanton for her editing, and typing of this manuscript. I also am deeply indebted to Jon Rieley Goddard for adding his professionalism in the editing process and for his ongoing and long friendship.

Introduction

I have always wondered how the Bible's words could have so much power. Somehow just being told that the Holy Spirit inspired the work did not answer my questions. I wanted to know how the actual words could leave such an impression. I had felt the power of those words, and on many occasions had seen others dramatically changed by reading those words. There had to be some trace in this world that would show how this transformation happens. It seemed to me that taking some of the mystery out of the writing would also simplify the task of understanding. There was a secret code that I wanted to know. When I first discovered that I could crack the code, I was so excited that I could hardly stand the suspense. Was the same code used all through the Bible? Was it understandable? I have taken representative styles of writing from the entire Bible to demonstrate that the code is used throughout. The code is broken and explained here. Each type of writing is different, and to understand the code different approaches had to be used. Each approach is described in this book.

This book is written to show ways in which you can be transformed spiritually by how you read the scriptures. It is designed to stimulate your relationship to God and the Bible in ways that open new possibilities for deepening your understanding and walk with God. I believe that by letting the Bible interpret itself to us, we do the best job of understanding the text. I am inviting us to allow the text to show us a new way to read and comprehend the text. While I may or may not adequately capture how best to describe methods and mindsets to read the Bible from, I believe emphatically that the text can give us clues on ways to best receive from it.

Even if you adopt this type of understanding about scriptures, it does not erase or decrease anything that you have received in the past.

This is only another way to allow scriptures to open themselves to us through understanding a bit more about the language and style in which they are written.

None of the suggestions for how to read the text are about the message the text gives. None of the suggestions in this book are meant to contradict any theological approach. These suggestions and information merely gives other ways to understand, interpret, appreciate, and experience the scriptures.

Using the method listed in this book does not require using or learning hypnosis. It means letting yourself read the Bible in ways that will contribute to your health, happiness, and understanding. Rather than a how-to book, this is more of a how-to-let-it-happen book. It is a book that explains how to sit back and let the power of the scriptures enter your life.

The details of analysis allow us to appreciate the ways scripture incorporates devices more powerfully than if we simply noted the surface meanings of words. Each text is examined and referenced in three ways to show how the scripture employs healing devices. The first reference notes the details beside each scriptural passage. A second shows a more complete use of various devices. The third reference is metaphorical, using stories from women in prison. Since those who wrote the Bible often communicate indirectly, I have attempted to adopt this style of writing as well. The women's stories are true; these stories provide a different perspective on the text. It is hoped that the stories will also give the reader ideas for life and work from a new perspective. I chose the illustrations carefully in order to stimulate thinking.

When I was a prison chaplain, I noticed that the female prisoners in my congregation were able to see through other people's actions. They needed, wanted, and required that scripture be relevant to them, and they sensed when people tried to use scripture to belittle, cause guilt feelings, control, or manipulate them. These women were willing to receive the messages of scripture and recognize what was being said between the lines. For example, the average prostitute learns to survive by being able to read people. Almost every prostitute can share a story about a time when she was almost killed by some crazy patron. Drug addicts and bad-check writers are also astute about seeing through people. In order to lie, they acquire the skill of reading others. Women who have taken a life usually are introspective because they are continuously examining their past actions. "s a result, these individuals are very sensitive to what others imply about them. Most folks in regular congregations can also read people well. While they may not possess these skills for survival reasons, living honestly enhances their ability to recognize what is being communicated. As well as survival skills, one other main difference between the prison and any other congregation is that the incarcerated are often more willing to ignore the niceties of social interaction. In other words, they are more willing to say it if a sermon stinks. If I have become a better preacher, it is because these women required me to grow, and they were kind enough to give me persistent feedback and allow me to make the necessary changes.

At some point, it became clear to me that the women in prison needed more than what I was giving. They were not responding to Bible studies in the usual sense. They were relying on their head-knowledge about the Bible, and this type of surface information was not producing good morals, impacting daily choices, or bringing about changes. Instead, it became a way of keeping themselves from integrating biblical information. I also realized that preaching to the inmates about what they should and should not do only served to irritate them or invite surface-level agreement. Loading a sermon with shoulds and oughts does not produce healing changes. The average woman in prison has so much guilt, shame, and remorse that she cannot hold much more. When a cup is full, it is full. Besides, guilt seldom produces positive changes, and when the guilt feeling wears off, usually the individual wants to protect herself from the church that failed to help her.

As a result of my experience, I began searching for answers. I knew that many of the women were hurting and that therapy from a psychodynamic perspective did not have much impact. By self-admission, two-thirds of women in prison have been abused. The actual figures are most likely higher because many women do not perceive what happened to them as abuse. This is either because it was seen as acceptable behavior by those around them, or as a child they said yes to an adult who manipulated them into agreeing to sex. Seeing their pain, and knowing that other effective therapies existed, was frustrating for me.

A counseling supervisor encouraged me to learn the techniques of Milton H. Erickson, MD, a man who is often referred to as the father of modern hypnosis. Erickson's approaches to helping people were unusual and radical ones that worked. Hopeless individuals became better, and uncooperative inmates became model prisoners. In short, Erickson's approaches provided me with new ways to help, and I incorporated his approaches in every aspect of my work as a chaplain. I was impressed with Erickson's compassionate, respectful attitude toward people. Erickson's caring methods allowed me to easily integrate these methods with theology because of the high level of respect for the client. He refused to offer any personality theories. Instead, he insisted that each person be approached as an individual.

When I started preaching at the women's prison, I was unsure of how to construct a sermon, and I had no idea of how to interpret a sermon's content. While I had knowledge that I had been taught in seminary, my understanding was limited to the imitation of sermons I had heard. It was not until a local minister, who out of the kindness of his heart was helping me to construct a sermon, that my understanding began to take shape. Since at the time I was also studying hypnosis, I began to comprehend sermons at a new level. At the same time, National Public Radio was airing a special on the sermons and speeches of the Rev. Martin Luther King Jr. Listening to King's sermons placed everything I was learning in context. King used hypnotic devices in artistic ways. Suddenly I understood that effective sermons used hypnotic devices that impacted listeners' emotions. In this way, lives could be changed. I set out to learn as much as I could about Erickson's therapy and hypnosis. I admit that after 19 years of practice, I still seek this learning.

These techniques can enhance your life's work. For instance, simply visiting someone in the hospital, and praying with him or her, imparts acceptance, worth, and importance. You are seeking to convey that you care about the person and want to evoke a sense of God's presence so they can receive the blessing, comfort, and hope that is found in God's presence. In part, this is accomplished when you prepare your own mind by becoming focused with scripture, prayer, or self-study, to name a few. When you eventually approach the hospital room, you are already filled with an emotion you hope to evoke for that individual. While you want to be responsive to the person's situation, a focus on God will be helpful regardless of what he or she is facing and whether or not you speak your thoughts about God to the person.

Have you ever made a visit that you did not want to make or spent time with someone you did not want to be near? Most of us have at some time tried to fake enthusiasm, interest, or compassion for people. In these situations, we can fool ourselves if we believe that we are getting away with being slick and covering our feelings. The average congregation might refrain from telling us; however, schizophrenics, paranoid folk, drug addicts, and prostitutes, to name a few, can see right through us. They will also often tell us about ourselves, and sometimes very directly. It is important to note that hypnosis does not cover disingenuous motives, actions, or words, or serve as a substitute for any kind of relating that is dishonest. If anything, using hypnosis invites an even more honest response because it provides no way for us to hide our actions from ourselves.

The hypnotic devices contained in language can be used to communicate effectively, rather than just logically. Since written words are multi-dimensional, hypnotic devices can be used to increase the available levels of language. The stories of the Bible and the parables of Jesus show how the use of healing language and poetry are related, because the gestalt of a story is more than just the words used. The gestalt of a story is the way in which the words are used to interact with us in our situations. We are invited into a powerful new manner of thinking, feeling, and seeing.

Honesty has tremendous impact. People can recognize, sense, and accurately identify motivations that they attribute to honesty. They can also correctly notice and detect dishonesty. They may have private reasons for not publicly acknowledging dishonesty, but they usually see it. Hypnotic language can enhance what is already being done in an honest way. In a parable, if the message is only stated on one level in a straightforward manner but not also implied on a different level in a different manner, the reader does not receive the invitation for internal change and thus does not receive the power of the emotional and spiritual discovery of truth.

Discovering the healing nature of scripture has been a significant, life-changing event for me. One of the many ways that it has impacted me is by giving me permission to use hypnotic devices without feeling manipulative or dishonest. I have found that it is a simple way of being even more intentional about what I hope to accomplish. I trust that the information listed in this book can also inspire you to receive more meaningful revelations when you read scripture. It is not meant to be the last word on the subject but an invitation for you to explore further. Perhaps by understanding my appreciation of hypnosis, you can begin to notice how you are already doing many of these things. When you become even more intentional, you can also be even more effective.

There is only one reservation I want to give the reader who thinks that using hypnotic techniques will bring them recognition as an outstanding preacher. While using these techniques may be helpful, effective, and healing to the congregation, using these techniques is not likely to convince others that you preach especially well. People hearing you may recognize that you love well, and they may notice more about who you are. They also may feel inspired and even become more fascinated with scripture, but becoming an exceptional preacher, or communicator, depends entirely on you.

Hypnosis in many religious circles is a bad word. The term has been misunderstood to mean the removal of personal power and the coercion of behavior. For others even more fearful, it represents the demonic. These individuals are usually unwilling to study or even attempt to comprehend hypnotic techniques. It is understandable that some people hold these attitudes given the minimal efforts that have been made to explain hypnosis in non-offensive ways. Literature is scant on books written about hypnosis and faith. Some preachers take jabs at hypnosis, either implying or saying directly that hypnosis is evil or bad.

Books about hypnosis are generally written for and read by people who already believe that hypnosis is a useful tool for ministry, therapy, medicine, or sports. Those who do not support the use of hypnosis seldom read books related to the subject.

Certain groups that use hypnosis aid in giving it an intolerable name. Groups associated with strange phenomena, witchcraft, spiritualism, or alien spacecraft add to the sense that hypnosis is something to avoid. Stage hypnotists use hypnosis for entertainment and contribute to the impression of the removal of personal power. Some movies use hypnosis as a devise to heighten suspense and even to support a rationale for bizarre killings. Both of these groups add to the misconception that hypnosis involves taking away personal choices against our will.

If hypnosis could take power away from people and use it in coercive ways, it would be appropriately defined as an evil force. Fortunately, this is not the case. In a hypnotic trance state, individuals cannot be forced into any action that they would be unwilling to perform in a non-trance state. A person can actually use resources that they were unaware that they possessed in a non-trance state. These unrecognizable, positive resources have always been a simple part of their overall living skills. In fact, until experiencing hypnosis, most people do not recognize that their own skills can be used for solving specific problems. For example, people may be able to quit smoking or overcome test anxiety through hypnosis because they already have the ability to do so. This occurs even when they are unaware of how to access their resources. Hypnosis serves as a vehicle for uncovering one's own positive resources.

It is an important fact that what we carry in our hearts or allow our minds to dwell upon does become part of what informs us during self-induced trance states. If during non-trance periods we harbor a deep grudge against another, that anger can be revealed during a drug-induced or spontaneously triggered trance state and become mis-directed. In such instances, hypnosis does not direct that type of trance. Evil does not originate from outside of us and our control but instead is found within us where we willingly choose the thoughts to be cultivated.

Jesus spoke very eloquently about this idea of where evil comes from. Jesus said in Matthew 15:19-20, "For out of the heart come evil thoughts, murder, adultery, fornication, theft, false witness, slander. These are what defile a man (person); but to eat with unwashed hands does not defile a man (person)." In Mark 7:20-23, Jesus said, "What comes out of a man (person) is what defiles a man (person). For from within, out of the heart of man (person), come evil thoughts, fornica-tion, theft, murder, adultery, coveting, wickedness, deceit, licentious-ness, envy, slander, pride, foolishness. All these evil things come from within, and they defile a man (person)." It seems clear that Jesus was convinced that what we think, dwell upon, and hold in our hearts either contaminates or purifies us.

Trance States

Being in a trance state is natural. We move in and out of trance states many times daily. Becoming engrossed in a TV program or a good book, or daydreaming are trance states. When we are so focused on problem-solving that we ignore obvious solutions, we are also in a trance state. Because this state is merely a condition of focused attention, it is natural. There are a number of theologians who believe that we are most in touch with God when we find ourselves totally consumed in the moment.

Dwelling on either positive or negative things can produce a trance state. We make the decision whether to feed ourselves spiritually healthy ideas or unhealthy worldly ideas. Concentrating on a subject can place the idea in our mind for later memory. This concept of recall is used repeatedly in advertisements. Have you ever noticed the brands of products that children request who watch TV? Often they use the identical rationale that has been given to them in commercials. These children may deny that commercials have had any influence over their lives. Like these children, we can also defend our position while keeping a straight face, wearing our brand clothing, and eating our name-brand cereals. Our choices are rationalized by our statements that certain products are better.

Ideas that we place in our unconscious do impact what is revealed during focused times of attention. Repeated practice of a piece of music or performance of a task can serve to inspire the reproduction of a practiced effort without much concentrated thought. Repetitive hearings and practice do have an impact on how we spontaneously accomplish tasks. This performance is most notable in the heat of an emotion or crisis.

Hypnotic language can be used to manipulate, communicate, or encourage in the same ways as other forms of communication. Language, or the style of language, is not necessarily good or bad. It is merely a form of communication. Good and moral preachers as well as immoral and evil people all use hypnotic language. Most are simply unaware that effective preaching almost always uses hypnotic communication. Instead of describing these preachers as hypnotic, we instead distinguish them as individuals who have a powerful impact on our lives, thinking, and emotions. In other words, we think of them as having charisma.

Most of us realize at some point that we are being influenced or directed, even if we deny it. We may be too embarrassed to admit that we are being tricked, but ultimately we know. We may choose to go along with a hypnotic influence because of personal reasons, and we may or may not ever reveal what we have noticed. Sometimes this occurs so that we can avoid some responsibility and later blame someone else. Other times, since it is positive, we remain willing to allow the directive. Coaches, teachers, therapists, and preachers may be allowed continuing authority because it serves as a positive influence for helping us to achieve our goals. Even slow or retarded people ultimately know if an intent of hypnosis is to help or hurt them.

The following church service experience emphasizes this point. While in Seminary, I took a unit of Clinical Pastoral Education where I worked in a hospital for the severely and profoundly retarded. The residents on my ward possessed such a level of retardation that they could not convey information through speech. The irony was that they communicated profoundly and taught me much. One Sunday the Catholic Sister in charge of the wing assembled the entire ward for a worship service that I was expected to lead. Every resident was placed around the edge of the room. They were clean and eager with anticipation. Their grunts, guttural sounds, and squeals were intimidating. As I began the story about Job, one very pretty and unhappy little girl began to cry. As she cried, the other residents became agitated. I knelt down next to her wheelchair, which was small to accommodate her tiny size, and I began to speak softly and lovingly toward her.

I knew that she was in pain because of the brace she had to wear while sitting in her wheelchair. I felt sad with my inability to help her, and I desperately wanted to provide some comfort because her pain was so evident. I mentioned to her that she was right, that Job had also been in pain, and that God had heard his despair and had helped him. In a similar way, I said, I wished for her to feel better. She instantly stopped crying. It was as if the entire room stood still in silence. Every eye became focused on both of us. When I I extended my sincere hope for healing to the others, every person gave me their undivided attention. In fact, throughout the remainder of the service, the little girl seemed comfortable and the other patients remained absolutely transfixed in their attention. Once the service was over, pandemonium resumed as usual.

Regardless of how this experience is interpreted, it was a profound one for me. I received the highest compliment possible in preaching when every resident paid attention. They intuitively knew that I cared about the little girl and, therefore, them. These patients could not have been tricked. Severely retarded people seem to accurately detect how people feel toward them. This may not necessarily be the way a person states that they feel. In this case, the residents understood that I cared, and they responded.

I believe that the emotional trance that we experienced in this event was one of being open to God's message. It spontaneously impacted all of us. The little girl's reduction of pain caused a powerful trance in us all. In the same way that her obvious pain elicited a profound concern from us, her pain in its leaving also significantly impacted us. Strong emotions, or significant spiritual events, have the capacity to impact those who are present. All of us have encountered the shared emotion of an athlete's success, or the sorrow of a team's loss after valiantly competing. Those emotions are a way of seeing the event. The winning team is happy because of the same event that evoked sadness in the losers. Perhaps this is not the manner in which most of us think about trance and yet it is a legitimate way to understand those events. If trance is defined as an altered state of focused attention, then the people rooting for both teams can equally be in a trance state while watching the same event yet having a profoundly different experience. The reason that both sides have a distinctive experience is, of course, that they have different ways of explaining the same events. This is a true statement of all trances whether naturally induced or guided by a hypnotist. We always have the ability to interpret our experience in unique ways. When in trance, we tend to rely on the ways we have understood reality in the past. Trance logic however, is different than normal-state logic.

The retarded residents repeatedly taught me that nonverbal communication is powerful. I also learned that regardless of how retarded a person is, or we perceive them to be, they can sense how we feel. One hydrocephalic child had to hold his eye open to see because his head was so swollen. In spite of this condition, he did not seem to be experiencing pain, and was quite playful about how he treated others. This boy was also unable to speak words. When people approached his bed and appeared to sincerely care about him, he would hold his eye open to see them clearly. If he detected phoniness, he would simply allow his eyelid to close and end his attention. I observed his interpretations of people to be very accurate. On several occasions I watched people approach his bed that were sincere, and he paid attention. When others were a bit phony in their concern, he would not force himself to overlook their phoniness. The child would simply release his eyelid and close them out of his world.

I have seen similar recognition of genuineness at the women's prison where I served as a chaplain. Flowery words seem only to impress the person who says them. A poor example of a con is a person who is so retarded by his own denial that he tries to manipulate others. I have watched guest preachers who have failed to notice that the inmates were acutely aware of their manipulative, thinly disguised self-aggrandizement. In these instances, inmates usually clap and make noise at the appropriate times in order to expose the preacher's facade. Occasionally different women said, "Can you believe that preacher? He actually thinks that he's fooling people." At other times, the inmates intentionally caught my eye while shaking their heads, or gave me a knowing look of disdain.

No amount of hypnosis or eloquent words can compensate for a lack of caring. Fashion, politics, and show cannot overcome the truth. People know when they are being conned and will realize this fact regardless of how slick the presentation. It may take time, but ultimately they recognize what is really happening and make a decision whether or not to play. In some cases, individuals may feel powerless to speak up for themselves.

On the other hand, even a boring, poorly spoken, and politically and fashionably inept speaker can be inspiring if we know that the person exerting a trance cares deeply for us and wants us to succeed. Hypnosis merely helps people to become more effective and/or more powerful in communicating. It is a way for us to be intentional about what we want to communicate while realizing that it may be difficult for others to receive our message.

For instance, how do we communicate forgiveness to a person who feels guilty? Can the words "you are forgiven" be said with much impact? Usually when a person is feeling guilty and someone says these words, he/she will be polite and say "thanks" but continue to hold feelings of guilt. Jesus is the only one who could use this phrase and have his forgiveness received. The rest of us have more difficulty in conveying this message. In order to have some impact, the communicating of forgiveness must be done in a sincere, indirect manner. Think about the times you have been forgiven by someone. A powerful trust results when forgiveness is communicated through acceptance, or by demonstrating a renewed trust. When we see or feel proof through the actions of others, we often receive the message of forgiveness.

It was because I realized how impotent I was in helping women in prison to feel forgiven, clean, or even hopeful that I began to study hypnosis. One of my clinical supervisors, who had been in the ministry for many years, encouraged me to explore whether hypnotic language might be useful in helping people feel forgiven. We both shared the frustration of saying, "You are forgiven" but not knowing whether it was accepted. It was difficult for me to believe that my message was heard if there was a glazed look on a person's face. My interpretation of their facial expression was, "No way."

A message that is implied rather than stated seems to have the greatest impact on people. This is illustrated by the following story. For years, a woman who was the unofficial Chaplain of the Seminary oversaw Louisville Presbyterian Seminary's bookstore. Lelia Rhodes made it a point to know every incoming student. She would often greet each new student by saying with enthusiasm and genuine positive regard; "You must be _____, I recognize you from your picture. It is good to meet you." Lelia was always warm, accepting, and understanding. She made each person feel that they were special to her. Perhaps it was because she honestly did think that they were special. Lelia lived her faith and communicated her appreciation for others. It was always a joy to be in her presence. On many occasions, her uplifting words were a warm welcome to whoever came into the bookstore. When classes or life in general had gotten some student down, Lelia's presence served as an encouragement. This was my experience. While she never directly said the words, "I believe in you," Lelia, with her actions, spoke them to me indirectly. It was her manner that allowed me to actually believe them. Lelia ministered in the same way to others, and had the same pastoral effect of helping them to trust in themselves.

Communicating forgiveness or acceptance is very similar to communicating compassion or helping a depressed person. Simply telling a person who is depressed to cheer up is not effective. The Book of Proverbs states that this type of comment is actually irritating to them. In order to help a depressed person move to a different way of understanding the world, we must first understand that depression is a self-imposed trance that an individual is unaware of inducing in themselves. Telling someone to cheer up ignores this point and is insulting. If the depressed person knew how to cheer up, he/she would. Helping the depressed person to gradually alter how he/she views the world is more useful. I found this to be true when using the Bible as a tool. When reading the Bible, I was able to comprehend the subtle shifts occurring between the lines of the text. The Book of Ecclesiastes is one text that has had a profound effect on me. While studying Ecclesiastes, I realized that the writer was as depressed as I was. Through my own process of identification, I knew that I was acceptable, even in my depression. In fact, I felt both encouraged and excited. The thinking and wisdom of the great writer of Ecclesiastes was similar to my own. I discovered that depressed thinking is depressed thinking and that this thought process most often involves similar conclusions. This identification coupled with implied messages of noticing these similarities helped me to once again feel hopeful.

Almost everyone shares the experience of being told, "Don't worry." Has this statement ever helped you to stop worrying? I doubt it. You may have pretended to agree but refrained from saying any more about your concerns. The words themselves do not provide much comfort. If we could easily stop worrying, we would. Words used in hypnosis, however, are effective in helping us to let go of unwanted feelings. This is partly done in an indirect way that is respectful of a person and of his/her perceived abilities. The Bible contains many suggestions about coping and dealing with anxiety. The ring of hypnotic language is usually heard in many of these indirect ways.

Perhaps the reasons people in some religious traditions have been afraid of hypnosis are because of the individuals who are associated with using hypnosis. Another explanation may involve associations that have made between hypnosis and psychiatry, or psychology. Hypnosis also may have generated a negative image because of stage hypnotists. Naming a culprit is guesswork. What is clear is that hypnosis and religion have a strained relationship. One of the places this tension is best seen is in the arenas where religious groups use hypnotic tools and treat their subjects with disdain.

While many readers of Mary Baker Eddie's work have seen connections between hypnosis and Christian Science, Ms. Eddie seemed to intentionally distance herself from mesmerism, or hypnosis. It is interesting that after spending time with Ms. Eddie, historians have noted similarities between Ms. Eddie's work and that of hypnotists of her day. Regardless of whether Ms. Eddie learned from early hypnotists, her attitude remained a distant one from hypnotism. She clearly believed that this connection was negative for the church.

There are people today who still hold the belief that any association between the church and hypnosis is negative. According to such individuals, hypnosis is unnecessary if we really believe in the power, or spirit, of God. They seem to believe that appreciating one means not liking or using the other. Hypnosis for them is interpreted as diminishing their faith or diluting the power of God. I believe that because God is so awesome and wonderful, we would never be able to diminish God or God's word by our study of hypnotic language. In addition, attempting to make God so small as to need protection is not in our best interest. Hypnosis has been a part of the Bible, faith, and of believers' experience from the beginning. Intentionally using these principles from hypnosis helps us to feel closer to God while enhancing our experience of the Holy.

People all over the world have sought ways to either move closer to God or to manipulate God into doing their bidding. They have used a variety of devices and contorted their bodies to heighten their senses to receive God's messages. People have both literally and figuratively whipped themselves into a state of frenzy to receive God's revelation. Some have gone without food or put themselves through mental and physical tortures. Others have used drugs, rituals, or embellishing movements to evoke God's spirit. These methods have also been used in attempts to coerce God into performing specific tasks. From the beginning of time, people have sought ways to experience God's presence or to entice God to perform actions.

All of these methods involve the creation of a trance. Any state of altered experience, by definition, is a trance state. While this is true, not all trance states are spiritual. When a trance state is defined as a state of focused attention, it is easy to see how performing rituals, fasting, or being completely still are natural. On the other hand, addictions and compulsions also fall into this category, even though they are not spiritual. There are positive and negative trance states that we encounter regularly. Understanding these conditions as trance states actually makes them easier to alter and manage.

Rituals that are performed well help to evoke a remembered state of awe, peacefulness, safety, and/or experience of God. Rituals focus our attention on the Holy. Rituals remove us from our everyday circumstances, and help us to anticipate what is to come while preparing for it. Rituals are common in both our everyday lives and in the worship services that we attend. Sitting in the same pew, arranging ourselves in an exact position, and praying identical prayers are examples of rituals.

Fasting is an example of a ritual that helps to produce a trance state. Fasting involves focusing our attention on abstinence from food while either attending to or attempting to ignore the physical, constant reminders from our bodies. These physical sensations serve as a focal point. While fasting for a day, we begin to change how we experience each moment, and our ordinary activities. If the purpose of our fast is to become closer to God, then throughout the day we will become more likely to anticipate and experience God's presence. Centering our attention on the physical will serve our purpose of focusing on the Holy. It is important to note that going without food in order to lose weight does not necessarily produce a positive experience. A person's desire to experience and center their attention on the Holy is required in order to produce a desirable trance state. Hunger produces a state of focused attention on food but not necessarily on God. Remaining still or concentrating on being motionless can also produce a light trance state. This is due to the fact that the sensation of remaining still becomes a focal point while the mind is absorbed in the act of staying motionless. Similar to fasting for weight loss alone, remaining still will not produce a positive trance without an intentional direction and/or a desire to achieve a closer relationship with God.

Herbert Benson, MD, studied practices of relaxation and meditation throughout the world. He discovered four qualities consistently found in the forms of relaxation. Regardless of whether the technique was Jewish, Christian, Buddhist, or any other, these four conditions were necessary for true relaxation. In many respects, the relaxation that Dr. Benson noted could also be considered a trance. The four criteria were as follows: 1) Quiet environment; 2) Mental device; 3) Passive attitude; and 4) Comfortable position.

A quiet environment is defined as a place where either the noise level is high enough to allow us to be alone with our thoughts or quiet enough for distraction-free thinking. Moving into a trance involves an atmosphere with this same type of silence. Actually, trances can be more easily developed with the luxury of distraction-free time, but trances do not necessarily depend upon this time.

A mental device can include a word, phrase, spot on the wall, candle, breath, or feeling. It involves anything that can be held, heard, experienced, said, or seen. Something that helps our mind narrow its point of focus is the only requirement. The Catholic rosary is a perfect example of a device that uses several of these mental devices at the same time. The focal point becomes tactile while relating to both time and position. This religious ritual involves simultaneously holding a rosary and reiterating mental words while praying repetitious prayers. Unfortunately for many Catholics, saying the rosary is associated with punishment rather than a deep relaxation that can lead to profound moments of peacefulness.

In a similar fashion, Jewish skullcaps, phylacteries, and prayer shawls can be used as effective tools to center attention. These resources use physical objects in order to recall certain peaceful, meditative moments when we have felt especially close to God. Ritualistic prayers are yet another type of instrument. An English speaking person who speaks ritualistic prayers in Hebrew can derive this same result of producing a trance. Prayer in the Jewish tradition involves remembering former times when God was helpful to Israel. This type of meditation today can help us to experience God's closeness.

Greek prayer beads, Russian Orthodox Icons, and Islamic prayer rugs, caps, and prayers all help to center attention in ways that invite a state of relaxation. The intensity of African American music, rhythm, and rhetoric in preaching also serves to invite a trance. While each of these examples is more ethnically or religiously oriented to a particular people, they are all excellent devices. We can attend these types of services and feel closer to God simply because our intentions are focused.

In Benson's study, a passive attitude is defined as being receptive to receiving revelation, insight, or relaxation. These are times when we are open to whatever thoughts enter our minds. Usually while we are dwelling on a mental device, the solution to a perceived dilemma will appear. At other times, less desirable thoughts intrude on our peacefulness. When the latter occurs, we are to passively allow them to drift rather than forcefully fight them with our precious, conscious attention.

Benson's comfortable position is defined as any stance that can be maintained for 20 minutes. Often prone positions can lead to sleep rather than trance or deep rest. Continuous movements are also effective for relaxation and trance states. Any long distance runner has experienced the peacefulness of both rest and trance. Many other sports also produce these opportunities for trance to develop spontaneously, either through repetitive movements or an intensity of attention.

Both athletes and spectators can effectively use the following games to develop trances: baseball, tennis, basketball, football, soccer. In these instances, the emphasis is on the intensity of the concentration in order to help develop both mini-trance states, and overall trance. Rituals surrounding shooting baskets or hitting a ball, for example, are used to evoke a sense of focused concentration for enhanced accuracy. Golf pros teach people to maintain a consistent pre-swing routine. When a player is under pressure, this pre-swing routine can actually evoke a sense of calm and help the player to follow through with a smooth swing.

Individuals who desire a perpetual closeness with God can use these same techniques. Evoking nearness to God is both more certain and more simple than producing a home run or even a base hit. Unfortunately, we seldom think of being able to invite God into our everyday lives. Consequently, very few of us realize how easy it can be to awaken our sense of peace and security through our relationship with God. This trance is accomplished by using routine tools that can also enhance sports performance.

For believers, God is always present.; it is also true that we are not continually aware of the presence of God. Trance does not involve bringing God close for selfish purposes. Instead, trance is a matter of opening our awareness to the fact that God is present with us. Similar to our breathing, God is always here. It is natural for us to become so focused on other things that we are unaware of our breathing. When some incident causes us distress, or someone provokes us to think about our breathing, we then become aware of our breathing.

The word "sacred" in Hebrew means to set aside for a special purpose. When we place a particular Bible away to be read only when we desire to deepen our relationship with God, simply touching that book will evoke openness to hearing God's word. By keeping a particular Bible sacred, it becomes a helpful tool for awakening feelings of awe and openness. While God is always with us, our experience of God ebbs and flows and is dependent upon our awareness at any particular moment. Using a tactile device such as a Bible, rosary, or cross aids us in our intentional worship, prayer, or meditation. A tactile device also induces a light trance of focused attention on God.

The Interpreter's Dictionary defines trance as "the state of mind of one who is receiving revelation." This is an appealing definition.

Recalling God's Word or mighty acts helps to elicit a state of mind where the peace of closeness becomes available in the moment. Despite the fact that we may have been previously unable to force these peaceful emotions, the act of focusing the attention on scripture or on times when God was near, helps us feel the presence of God.

Psalm 77 uses this same form. Given the fact that the writer is experiencing feelings of distress, forlornness and abandonment, the writer attempts to meditate on or become closer to God. The writer begins this process by recalling what God has done for Israel in the past. Verse 11 says, "I will call to mind the deeds of the Lord: yea, I will remember thy wonders of old." It is interesting that within a short period of time, the writer is recalling God's deeds and beginning to speak in a more upbeat manner. We can certainly learn from this pattern. When we find ourselves feeling rejected, we can also choose to remember God's merciful acts and those specific moments when we felt nearer to God. In terms of hypnotic language, this is defined as pace and lead. Pace (acknowledging emotions of despair) and lead (recalling the feelings of awe or closeness to God) is accomplished by recalling those moments when Israel was near. Much of the Psalms are filled with this style of writing. That is, capturing certain feelings common to all us. When we can identify with a particular author's emotions, we can also acknowledge that we are acceptable.

I vividly remember reading Ecclesiastes when I was depressed. I felt disconnected from everyone, including God. Somehow, I held myself responsible for my depression. Since I was unaware of how my depression had originated, I also felt condemned. As I read Ecclesiastes, I realized that the author was more depressed than I was. With my new understanding, I began to experience both encouragement and acceptance. I interpreted Ecclesiastes' inclusion in the cannon to mean that my depression was not so horrific. In fact, I felt strengthened through my identification with the writer's thoughts. Depressed thinking recognizes other depressed thinking. Noting that the Book of Ecclesiastes functions regularly in this manner was a meaningful revelation for me.

Perhaps it is one of the purposes for the placement of this book in the cannon.

Whether the Bible is connecting with us emotionally, or giving us hope, inspiration, wisdom, or commandments, many of the Bible's authors have used indirect communication. A great number of these devices contained in the Bible are referred to as hypnotic. It is my intention to demonstrate the ways in which the Bible is hypnotic. I also plan to highlight various techniques for using Hypnotic language skills that will provide assistance to individuals in ministry.

Philippians

Paul's genuine focused attention and care for the gospel, for the Philippians, and for the Philippians' faith fill the Letter to the Philippians with hypnotic devices at every turn. In order for Paul to have loaded this letter with so many hypnotic devices, he had to be in a trance. Only from a state of such focused attention could Paul have written a letter that speaks simultaneously on so many levels. This involved Paul's total attention being given to his desiring the best for the Philippians while he encouraged them to spread the gospel. Paul obviously loved God; he must have also loved the Philippians. In this impressive letter, every verse in the first chapter contains at least one hypnotic device that Paul used to convey his message more powerfully.

Paul's original intent was not necessarily to use embedded positives. Paul was in fact deeply concerned about the Philippians, and it is apparent in his writing. Real caring cannot be faked or contrived, and we, like the Philippines, realize Paul's words are genuine. With the substance contained in these verses, it is easy for us to understand the inspired nature of this book.

Verse for verse, the second chapter of Philippians contains more hypnotic devices than most texts written by modern hypnotists. The number of unintentionally included devices is more numerous here than what can be found in similar, painstakingly crafted letters by other authors. Philippians is truly inspired in what is defined as a trance state. The work of Paul stands as a monument to honest, genuine caring for others. It also is symbolic of what real caring can accomplish when it is focused in a single-minded trance. We could state that Paul's single-minded attention and caring made straight the path of revelation. This is because his use of hypnotic language helps to remove the ordinary obstacles of everyday distractions. We could also say it in yet another way: the spirit was powerfully working in Paul's life when he wrote this book.

The following experience has aided in my understanding of how Paul's intentional caring directly influenced my work as a chaplain. One Christmas Eve, Dr. Catherine Johnson from Louisville Presbyterian Seminary came to the women's prison to help me with the services. In particular, she assisted me in providing a service for inmates who were locked down in their cells. Because regulations prohibited these women from gathering outside of their cells for church services, I took them each a service individually. This is similar to the Meals on Wheels concept of delivering both food and a blessing in person. Since we provided some of the only contact for these women in segregation, I was always intentional as I attempted to feel thankful for each woman and love her as best I humanly could through my faith. It was my hope to convey the idea of each woman's importance as I interacted with her in the cellblock. As Dr. Johnson accompanied me that Christmas Eve, she noticed my interactions with the inmates. She observed the genuine appreciation that these women exhibited in response to being remembered. Dr. Johnson said that she understood why I liked Philippians since my ministry in prison was based on Paul's work. I comprehended her statement to mean that I strived to communicate acceptance, value, and appreciation for these women. I believe that one of the reasons these inmates got themselves locked down was because they did not feel cared about and had acted out to express their dislike of themselves. I sincerely hope that I was disclosing to these women the importance of the scriptures and their relationship to God.

It is my hope that in our examination of Paul's work through the magnifying glass of hypnotic language, we can add respectful understanding to one way the spirit of God works. The numerous hypnotic language tools employed are ones that deserve our careful attention. This examination is so that we, as readers, can also be more effective in communicating our concerns and care for others.

The style of the language in Philippians is confusing. The numerous hypnotic devices are overwhelming and can be too numerous to catch on casual reading. Furthermore, there are embedded positive messages for the reader and numerous examples of implied meanings that are positive about the reader, the reader's future and what is possible for the reader, or believer. That is just one of the points of this text. The reader can learn from the scriptures a method of reading the scriptures that improves the reader's experience. If you were willing to let God speak to you throughout the process and in between the lines of Philippians, you could learn much and gain much for your spiritual walk.

If you read Philippians with the goal that you are going to trust God's word to simply wash over you and to fill you heart and mind with God's thinking, attitude and mindset, then you would be following the path that this text invites you to take. In the complexity and the number of positive messages and encouragements to trust that you would get, and which God wants you to receive, you can experience a new way of reading the text.

Philippians invites a different way of reading, listening, and experiencing the scriptures than do other styles of writing in the Bible. Philippians invites you to experience the message instead of remembering the message. Some forms of language styles in scriptures invite a head-and-heart experience. Some passages encourage a broader perspective, or one that is more urgent. If you went by what the hypnotic language structure of the passage most invites, then how you would read Philippians would be different from how you would read Genesis, the psalms or any other biblical passage. I believe that most folks who regularly read the Bible do this type of shifting without consciously thinking about having done it. One of the ways you can best draw from Philippians would be to let it simply wash over you and fill your senses with the meanings implied in the passage. Other types of writing invite other styles of listening to maximize what you receive from the passage. For example, attempting to read the Ten Commandments and just allow the messages to wash over you would miss the complexity and the beauty of the words. The Ten Commandments are better mediated on, considered, and thoughtfully understood. In contrast, one of the prominent ways to read the Psalms to maximize you experience is to identify with the emotional experiences described.

I believe that one of the reasons that people who do not have much experience reading the Bible seem to have so much difficulty getting anything out of the text is that they attempt to read the text as they would a novel, textbook, or cookbook. Reading Philippians for the first time as a textbook or instructional manual is not going to allow the same type of experience as reading it from the perspective of merely experiencing sacred words. Each of the styles of the text invites a different type of trance state that can best be used to draw out the linguistic blessings. It is only with practice, experience, or leadership that we learn more productive methods of reading scriptures.

Because of the compactness of the hypnotic devices in the text, one value of letting this book simply be accepted into your mind, and spirit without long considerations or thoughtful meditations is that you will likely feel better. You might not know how it is that you simply have a more positive attitude, but is very likely to happen.

Beginning with Philippians, I will examine many books of the Bible that employ the use of hypnotic language. The format for analyzing the text remains the same. Each verse is displayed to the left with its corresponding hypnotic devices shown to the right. An explanation of the devices is found after every two or three verses, as well as an illustration describing how the hypnotic tool is used in the specific verse.

1 Paul and Timothy, servants of Christ Jesus, To all the saints in Christ Jesus who are in Philippi, with the bishops and deacons. 2 Grace to you and peace from God our Father and the Lord Jesus Christ.	Introduction; pacing; implied compliment to the readers being saints or believers; rapport building; general greeting done well.

Paul grabs the readers' attention in these first two verses. We can almost feel the enthusiasm in this letter to all the saints. It is interesting that this letter is written to believers only. It is implied that the people reading this letter are believers since the compliments, blessings, and information are for these individuals. Although we as modern readers are not in Philippi, we still can receive Paul's blessing indirectly. Perhaps initially, we dismiss the introductory grace, or compliment, because we feel it does not apply to us. If we continue, however, we will find it difficult not to receive some of the embedded blessings and implied positive messages.

3 I thank God every time I remember you, 4 constantly praying with joy in every one of my prayers for all of you, 5 because of your sharing in the gospel from the first day until now.	In the third verse, implied message, rapport are being built. In verse four, implied message of liking you and feeling joy when you are thought of, also that you are prayed for daily. In verse five, implied positive remembrance and importance.

In the third verse, rapport is being built as the writer implies that the reader is important. The author communicates indirectly that the reader is thought of often and with importance. At this point, our interest is most likely being raised. In a similar way, the writer implies that we are liked in verse four. Thinking of us often, and with joy, is an effective attention grabber and a powerful implication. The author is continuing to build rapport. In verse five, the shared gospel binds us, like the Philippians, together. This important bond is implied. The writer also uses a simple conjunction, because, to link the inferred importance of thinking of us, with joy and the reasons we share in the gospel. As readers, we are told that we are important simply because we share in the gospel. This statement is a profound truth about intimacy and relationships. People who share the same beliefs develop a powerful bond.

6 I am confident of this, that the one who began a good work in you will bring it to completion by the day of Jesus Christ.	Implied message, positive expectancy, and continued rapport building; elicits expectancy; growth is presupposed.

That we, as readers, will continue to grow spiritually is a presupposed message in this verse. The author uses positive expectation.

Paul's confidence in God working for us is accepted as fact. It is also implied that good work is being performed both in and through the reader(s). Since the writer does not use a referential index, there is no ambiguity about what is being said. Without the referential index, however, we can easily read into the text whatever is occurring with us. This results in a more personalized understanding for the reader(s). For example, is it the good work being performed first in us and then through us? Or is it perhaps performed only in us? Maybe it is in us, but through us for other's benefit. It also could be in us and for us and also for others through us. Obviously God can be creating a good work in us, for others, and us, and through us, simultaneously. OK, perhaps I cannot do this as well as Paul. You understand the concept better, and have a sense of intuitively knowing. You probably knew even as you read the words that I was up to something in the above sentence.

7 It is right for me to think this way about all of you because you hold me in your heart, for all of you share in God's grace with me, both in my imprisonment and in the defense and confirmation of the gospel.	Pacing; implied care; implied return care; simple conjunctions; confusion. There are at least seven ideas connected together.

Even though cause and effect are not established in the seventh verse, the seven ideas that are strewn together with conjunctions, implied causatives, and logic invite us to agree with Paul. Several implied messages are found here that speak positively either toward the Philippians, Paul, or their faith combined. Their sharing in the gospel is interpreted as the Philippians' caring for Paul. Confusion results, however, in these seven ideas being strung together. How many people could actually remember what was being said or implied? As readers, we will find it difficult to deny the inferred positive messages that become virtually hidden. To complicate matters, what follows in verse eight is also positive. It is interesting that if the reader becomes confused by the seventh verse, then verse eight's positive message might be more readily accepted. Because the conscious mind is less likely to argue, the positive messages in the seven stacked ideas are more likely to be received at an unconscious level. While it is difficult to consciously block statements, we become more easily able to accept positive compliments because of being distracted by the confusion. This process occurs even when we normally reject compliments at a conscious level.

8 For God is my witness, how I long for all of you with the compassion of Christ Jesus.	Implied positive; pacing; reframe of his care that it comes from Christ.

The implied positive message is that Paul cares as deeply for the reader(s) as Jesus does. When three ideas are strung together in verse eight, it is perceived as if they all fit together. That God is Paul's witness does not make the statement in this verse true, but it directly follows the confusion found in verse seven. As readers, it almost becomes what we say to ourselves, following our confusion. Paul's longing also does not necessarily need to be connected with the idea of Christ's compassion. On the other hand, connecting the two ideas makes them dependent upon each other. For example, if we know that Paul cares for us, it is also implied that Christ longs for us. Paul's caring is interpreted as Christ's caring.

9 And this is my prayer, that your love may overflow more and more with knowledge and full insight 10 to help you to determine what is best so that in the day of Christ you may be pure and blameless, 11 having produced the harvest of righteousness that comes through Jesus Christ for the glory and praise of God.	Implied belief in the reader; confusion; seeding of ideas; implied instruction to be blameless; implied ability to make decisions; presumed attribute of love; simple conjunction of ideas with implied causatives.

The first implied message in this passage is that Paul prays for us, the readers. Secondly, Paul infers that we already feel love for others. The inherent confusion for the reader is due to the difficulty of the text. At least eight different messages are contained within this sentence. These concepts do not necessarily fit together. Simple conjunctions are used as connectors, but they do not help to explain the meaning of the ideas. There is also a lack of logic in the flow of these ideas. For example, the perception that love produces knowledge or insight may be true, but it does not naturally follow a rational scheme. There is the implied message that we can become pure and blameless by choosing to receive God's love. Because of the obscure way this idea is introduced, the reader can easily believe that the notion is being seeded. Paul only touches on the subject of righteousness coming through Jesus in this passage.

12 I want you to know, beloved, that what has happened to me has actually helped to spread the gospel,	Syntactic ambiguity, implied and encapsulated endearment; positive reframe; stacked and confusing sentence with 10 or more separate ideas.
13 so that it has become known throughout the whole imperial guard and to everyone else that my imprisonment is for Christ;	Simple conjunction linking ideas to establish more the perspective developed. Cause and effect also used in establishing frame.
14 and most of the brothers and sisters, having been made confident in the Lord by my imprisonment, dare to speak the word with greater boldness and without fear.	Implied and presupposed willingness to speak the word. Implied message to readers that they can alsospeak boldly without fear.

The 12th verse begins with a sentence that becomes ambiguous. "I want you to know" is followed by the endearment "beloved". Beloved can be understood as being only a word acknowledging the reader, or that the reader is beloved. The reader brings to the text his/her understanding of what beloved means. It is implied that the reader is interested in becoming bolder in his/her speaking. Similar to verses 9-11, this sentence, with its 10 or more separate ideas that are not necessarily connected, positively reframes Paul's circumstances from ones where he invites pity, sorrow, empathy, or sadness to those in which he rejoices. The positive outcome is attributed to Paul's circumstances even though a connection between the two may be difficult for the reader to determine.

15 Some proclaim Christ from rivalry, but others from good will.	Indirect suggestion to proclaim the Gospel; pacing.

That some proclaim Christ from rivalry would be congruent with the reader's experience. It is also true that some of us proclaim Christ from goodwill. This verse, therefore, is pacing the reader. Furthermore, the idea that the reader is to proclaim Christ is implied in this sentence and the ones that follow.

16 These proclaim Christ out of love, knowing that I have been put here for the defense of the gospel; 17 the others proclaim Christ out of selfish ambition, not sincerely but intending to increase my suffering in my imprisonment.	Indirect suggestion to proclaim Christ out of love; reframe of why Paul was in prison; pacing; negative reframe and implied overcoming of the attempt.

In this verse, there is no specification to whom "these" refers. We are left believing that Paul is either writing about us or someone else that we are to imitate. Regardless of our interpretation, the implied message is for us to proclaim Christ out of love. Paul's attitude toward his incarceration reframes positively what could be viewed negatively. In verse 17, we realize that there are people who proclaim Christ out of selfish ambition. This statement is congruent with the reader's experience. Paul proceeds to negatively ascribe the personal attack on him as the motive behind proclaiming Christ out of selfish ambition. The negative attribute infers that we, as readers, are to avoid this behavior. Paul also implies that such attempts have failed to increase his suffering and that he is immune to personal attacks. It follows that we do not need to be concerned about stopping these sorts of proclamations.

18 What does it matter? Just this, that Christ is proclaimed in every way, whether out of false motives or true; and in that I rejoice.	Rhetorical question that begins the reframe; presupposes the cause to be unstoppable; seeds the idea that spreading Gospel is very important

In this verse, Paul challenges us to use even negative reasons for presenting Christ. In fact, he blesses anyone who chooses to do so. Paul also implies that anyone who notices others proclaiming Christ even out of selfish motives can rejoice because Christ is being proclaimed. The Lord's hand is understood to be in the proclamation. Paul infers that even those individuals with impure motives are acceptable if they proclaim the gospel. How could someone whose motives are pure accomplish much more? Later in the letter, Paul develops this theme of encouragement for the reader to spread the word.

yes, and I will continue to rejoice 19 for I know that through your prayers and the help of the Spirit of Jesus Christ this will turn out for my deliverance. 20 It is my eager expectation and hope that I will not be put to shame in any way, but that by my speaking with all boldness, Christ will be exalted now as always in my body, whether by life or by death.	Implied causative; reframe reframed; implied power in their prayers that he knows are for him. Verse 20: Double bind; implied responsibility to assist in no shame to Paul especially to continue to pray and to see Christ exalted in Paul's life and/or death.

Paul's imprisonment is reframed in this passage as the thought of rejoicing is continued here from verse 18. The reader's prayers are implied as a future causative of Paul's deliverance in verse 19. These ideas are stacked on top of each other, making them difficult to separate. The same sentence infers both that there is power in our prayers and that we are praying for Paul. Regardless of whether readers are actually praying for Paul, positive and negative feelings are elicited. On one hand, we may feel good that this important man Paul appreciates our prayers. On the other hand, we may feel guilty that we have not been praying for Paul, and we may begin because we are held in such high regard. The implied power in our prayers, however, is still magnificent because it is implicitly rather than directly stated. There is a double bind given to us as readers to interpret what happens to Paul as occurring for the exaltation of Christ. All the contingencies are covered; Paul either lives or dies. We are encouraged to accept this worldview that encompasses both outcomes.

21 For to me, living is Christ and dying is gain. 22 If I am to live in the flesh, that means fruitful labor for me; and I do not know which I prefer.	Reframe; double positive bind; implied message that we all could be fruitful and that being fruitful is good.

Once again Paul's circumstances are framed as positive. By viewing both sides of the dilemma of living or dying as a positive, Paul has covered all contingencies. Implied messages include: to live is fruitful, to be fruitful is good, and people who are dedicated strive to be good.

23 I am hard pressed between the two: my desire is to depart and be with Christ, for that is far better; 24 but to remain in the flesh is more necessary for you.	At least distraction if not confusion; implied messages; overall continuation of reframe from verses above.

Verse 23 is written in a confusing way. The reframe, however, continues since both possibilities are good, regardless of what the future brings. In addition, the implied message is that Paul is alive now and perhaps in the future because of the reader(s). Also inferred is that both Paul and God deeply care and believe in the reader(s).

25 Since I am convinced of this, I know that I will remain and continue with all of you for your progress and joy in faith, 26 so that I may share abundantly in your boasting in Christ Jesus when I come to you again.	Confusion; implied message of readers' positive future and of Paul's living; directive to boast in what Christ has done given indirectly.

These two verses are confusing because so many ideas are included with a number of modifiers. When the author's use of the passive voice is included with these factors, it is easy to understand why this passage is particularly difficult to grasp. While previously, Paul revealed to us his ambivalence about remaining alive, he implies here that he will share joy with us in the future. We are promised that we will have joy and will be able to boast. Paul indirectly gives us a directive to boast about what the Lord has done for us.

27 Only, live your life in a manner worthy of the gospel of Christ, so that, whether I come and see you or am absent and hear about you, I will know that you are standing firm in one spirit, striving side by side with one mind for the faith of the gospel,	Direct suggestion; confusion; implied suggestion to stand firm in one spirit and one mind. This could also be understood as an indirect directive.
28 and are in no way intimidated by your opponents. For them this is evidence of their destruction, but of your salvation. And this is God's doing.	Implied message of "do not be afraid of your opponents." Reframe of how to see the current events.

In this sentence, the direct suggestion for us is clear: Live our lives. Confusion results, however, from Paul's inclusion of many different ideas, thoughts, and implied messages. Identifying these concepts is difficult. There are at least eight ideas contained in verse 27. This number does not include the implied messages or directives. For example, the author infers that we, with other believers, are to stand firm in one mind. Although as readers we could think of this statement as a suggestion, Paul's words contain the firmness of a directive. He intends for us to carry out these instructions. One remaining implied message to be noted is the idea that being of one mind is "for the faith of the gospel." Paul infers that this type of collective effort is appreciated by God and serves a greater purpose than merely getting along with other believers.

29 For he has graciously granted you the privilege not only of believing in Christ, but of suffering for him as well
30 since you are having the same struggle that you saw I had and now hear that I still have.	Reframe; implied message suffering for Christ is good and can be taken as a compliment. Verse 30: Confusion; rapport; implied message is we are very similar; the struggle is reframed to be a symbol of respect.

In verse 29, suffering is reframed as a condition in which we can take pride. In other words, we are worthy of receiving our pain. Implied is the message that we have been and are doing well. A secondary message is that belief and the ability to suffer are gifts. Verse 30 is complex. We as readers are linked together with Paul in the similarity of our circumstances. This is complimentary to us because we are seen as being as worthy as Paul. As a remembrance, we are given a symbol of respect for ourselves; we are like the evangelist Paul.

Exodus

The Ten Commandments can evoke guilt in most of us. This may involve simply bringing to our minds the realization that we do not know them by heart. Perhaps we only remember the ones that periodically bring us difficulty. If this is true for those of us not in prison, imagine how intense it can be for inmates who know that they have fallen short, and have broken vows and commandments.

People who are not associated with prison have difficulty comprehending the degree of guilt found in these institutions. During my initial years as a women's prison chaplain, I did not understand how fully inmates mask their pain. I remember talking with a young woman whose drunkenness resulted in the deaths of two small children. As we visited, I found myself feeling increasingly frustrated when this woman did not show any signs of remorse. Finally, I asked her how she could remain so calm about what she had done, especially since she had children of her own. The mask that she was wearing dropped, and she immediately began to sob. At this point, she was barely able to breathe from her distress. When her sobbing began to diminish to crying, she angrily turned to me with tears streaming down her face and said, "Chaplain, you have no idea what it is like. Each waking moment, I am aware of nothing else. I see those children in my mind, and I feel so bad. Most days all I experience is remorse and guilt. I try to hide it because nobody seems be able to deal with my pain." This woman taught me a valuable lesson. I now frequently notice this type of guilt and remorse. It is difficult for most of the women in prison to live with this penitence. People, who carry the guilt of taking another's life, live their lives in Hell. I understand there to be no other way of describing this experience for people who are not labeled as sociopathic. These are individuals who have made a terrible, irreversible mistake. In prison, one guaranteed way to evoke any inmate's guilt is by reading the Ten Commandments.

NRSV
Exodus 20:1-17

1 Then God spoke all these words:	Framing; pacing.
2 I am the LORD your God, who brought you out of the land of Egypt, out of the house of slavery,	Establishing rapport; reframing; indirect suggestion.
3 you shall have no other gods before me.	Directive; framing; creating drama.
4 You shall not make for yourself an idol, whether in the form of anything that is in heaven above, or that is on the earth beneath, or that is in the water under the earth.	Directive; indirect suggestion; symbol of problem.
5 You shall not bow down to them or worship them; for I the LORD your God am a jealous God, punishing children for the iniquity of parents, to the third and the fourth generation of those who reject me,	Directive; indirect suggestion; creating drama.
6 but showing steadfast love to the thousandth generation of those who love me and keep my commandments.	Indirect suggestion; interspersal; directive.
7 You shall not make wrongful use of the name of the LORD your God, for the LORD will not acquit anyone who misuses his name.	Directive; symbol; indirect suggestion, Creates frame.
8 Remember the Sabbath day, and keep it Holy.	Directive; directive.
9 Six days you shall labor and do all your work.	Directive; pace; indirect suggestion
10 But the seventh day is a Sabbath to the LORD your God; you shall not do any work—you, your son or your daughter, your male or female slave, your livestock, or the alien resident in your towns.	Indirect suggestion; directive; indirect suggestion.

11 For in six days; the LORD made heaven and earth, the sea, and all that is in them, but rested the seventh day; therefore the LORD blessed the Sabbath day and consecrated it.	Anecdotes; symbol; indirect suggestion
12 Honor your father and your mother, so that your days may; be long in the land that the Lord your God is giving you.	Directive; future orientation; indirect suggestion; indirect suggestion.
13 You shall not murder. suggestion.	Directive; indirect
14 You shall not commit adultery.	Directive; indirect suggestion.
15 You shall not steal.	Directive; indirect suggestion.
16 You shall not bear false witness against your neighbor.	Directive; indirect suggestion.
17 You shall not covet your neighbor's house; you shall not covet your neighbor's wife, or male or female slave, or ox, or donkey, or anything that belongs to your neighbor.	Directive; indirect suggestion.

Verse 1 frames the entire Exodus passage. God is speaking. This is important to note because God's words are more significant than, for example, Moses' or any other speaker's words. The rest of this passage is framed in this light. Since we are invited to accept the same frame of reference in which God is speaking, pacing is occurring. If we approve, then we accept the writer's pacing.

Verse 2 is one of only three verses in this text that are stated in the positive, in the English translation. Included with verse 2 are verses 8 and 12. It follows that the remaining verses in this passage are translated in the negative. Beginning with verse 2, the writer gives us a directive to have "no other gods before God." Because of the nature of this directive, there is also a framing of our relationship: God directs and we follow. The writer sets the stage for a drama, since he infers that people can choose to worship other gods. This tacit drama is one in which the worship of other gods plays a part. What is unclear, in this scene, is God's consequences for us if we choose to worship other gods.

Verse 3 states a negative directive to "not have other gods before God." It also frames, for us, how idolatry relates to the Ten Commandments. Any violation of the commandments is, in part, a breach of the Second Commandment. This type of violation is interpreted as putting our wants first. Consequently, it is an act of worshiping something or someone before God. As in verse 2, the writer uses a simple phrase to begin this creation of a drama. We, the audience, infer that things and people will be placed ahead of God. The mysterious unraveling of this scene is certainly a drama.

The Fourth Commandment further clarifies the Second Commandment with the author's specific statements that things can be placed above God. This explanation is also symbolic of the problem of idolatry. A negative directive is given, that we "not make" idols, and an indirect suggestion is given, that we "make" an idol. This inferred suggestion could be understood using the following example. With the statement to "not go" into the street, there is almost an unspoken compulsion to "go" into the street. Since the "not" is unrecognizable for the brain in a trance state, the hypnotic command becomes to "go" into the street.

Verse 5 gives a directive. "You shall not" is coupled with an indirect suggestion. This directive from the author to us is in order for us and our children, grandchildren, and future generations to avoid punishment. The fact that some of our difficulties arise from our ancestors' sinfulness is also implied here. This is an uncanny observation concerning one possible reason people convey emotional and psychological difficulties from one generation to the next. Again, a dramatic effect begins to form. With the degree of emphasis upon not worshiping idols, we are almost certain to be pulled into a struggle. That God specifically tells us that God would punish a violation of this commandment is also drama-inducing.

An indirect suggestion begins verse 6. The writer instructs us that in order to receive God's steadfast love, we must to obey God's commandments. The words "love me and keep my commandments" are used as both a directive and an interspersed command. The command is stated with the following main message: People who keep God's commandments will have God's steadfast love.

In verse 7, God's name is to be treated with such reverence that to make wrongful use of it is sin. The verse begins with the negative directive "you shall not," and then uses God's name as a symbol for God's being. The indirect suggestion is for us to be cautious about how we use God's name.

Verse 8 is one of the three positive directives within this decalog. The following two decrees are stated here: remember and keep holy. A positive directive is also contained in verse 9. The words "you shall labor" and "do all your work" fit these criteria. An indirect suggestion is given that anticipates verse 10's prohibition against work on the Sabbath. The verse 9 paces our experiences as working adults.

Verse 10 includes a directive, which is sandwiched between two indirect suggestions. "You shall not do any work" is this decree. The writer first states indirectly that we owe the Sabbath to the Lord. His second message is that we are to teach and enforce this commandment to all individuals whom we influence, including those in our household.

The writer uses an anecdote of creation in verse 11. He conveys to the reader an indirect suggestion that we are also to abide by, and keep the commandment that honors the Sabbath.

Verse 12 is another commandment positively stated by the author. The "honor thy" is a command/directive. The verse also orients us toward the future in two ways. First it refers to honoring our parents as leading to long life. More implicit is the idea that by honoring our parents, we may also be honored by our children. This is one of two indirect suggestions contained in this verse. The other one is that the Lord not only gives us land, but implicitly everything.

Verses 13-17 contain the same structure. In the English translation, the verses include both the directive "you shall not," and an indirective suggesting "you shall" commit the offense. In order to think of how to "not do" something, we first have to think of how to "do" it. These verses are examples of how one language cannot be translated accurately into another. In the Hebrew version, we find absolute prohibitions. There are no mixed signals. The English translation, on the other hand, does not adequately convey the completeness and finality of the prohibitions.

Regardless of whether we live in prison, reading the Ten Commandments evoke guilt. Inmates are painfully aware that they have not kept the commandments. If we are also honest with ourselves, we realize we all have broken the commandments. This remembrance can result in more than guilt. It brings with it the tremendous feelings of sorrow and worthlessness. There is also a sense of appreciation for forgiveness. The more we feel forgiveness, the more we experience appreciation. The difference between the prison and church is that prisoners usually feel more freedom to admit that they have violated the commandments. The adage that everyone in prison claims to be innocent is untrue. A few do claim to be innocent of their convicted charges. Usually the innocent ones become willing to recognize that they have committed other sins, regardless of whether these sins are illegal. The only inmates who continue to protest their innocence when their guilt is obvious are child abusers. Both physical and sexual child abusers have a much more difficult time in admitting their imperfections, sins, or crimes.

The Jewish and Christian perspectives on the commandments appear to be slightly different. For the Jew, thoughts are not a factor. For example, feeling angry enough to want to kill does not evoke the guilt of having broken a commandment. For the average Christian, these homicidal thoughts are interpreted as a violation. Both perspectives hold the common belief that no one can keep all 10. In addition, these perspectives also share the guilt associated with not keeping what God has commanded. How the guilt encourages us to act is a primary question. Are we motivated to sin more or to sin less? How does our guilt affect our relationship with God? While examining the commandments through hypnotic language typically raises more questions, this analysis can also lead to many answers.

A noticeable problem appears when we view the Ten Commandments through the eyes of hypnotic language. Most of the commands are stated in the negative. "You shall not steal" from a hypnotic standpoint, communicates "you shall steal." The brain fails to understand the "not" as part of the command. We all have the experience of wanting to "touch" something after being told, "don't touch." In this case, the subtle command was given to us to "touch." When I first observed this problem, I was shocked. I thought that either the translators or those people with hypnotic understandings were wrong.

I asked myself why the writers of the Bible chose to place the commandments in a negative context. With this style of writing, the commandments are difficult to follow. When the wording of the commandments is compared with other biblical texts, the contrast is obvious. The wording in the Psalms, for example, actually helps the reader to do what is being asked. In fact, throughout the Bible this style of writing serves as a tool for us to subtly gain wisdom. This also ultimately aids in our feeling better and gaining deeper knowledge.

It is ironic that the author of the commandments has chosen to use difficult linguistics, given the relevance of the commandments to our faith. This observation is especially curious considering that the commandments' overall message is so important. After pondering this idea, my questions were answered as I consulted the Hebrew translation. I discovered that the error was clearly found in the difficult translation of the total prohibition with a few words in English. Conveying the message in an effective way is simply not possible. Only in Hebrew can the total prohibitions of the commandments be stated with an economy of words. Our "Thou shalt not" is simply too weak to communicate the power and strength of the prohibition. In the Hebrew, a negative concept is not translated. Instead, a powerful prohibition is stated emphatically.

I believe that words are used intentionally in the Bible. A text's structure is revealing for us as it gives us wisdom. The framework of the Ten Commandments invites us to realize our dependency on God for forgiveness. Similar to how Abraham depended on his faith, the Ten Commandments invite us to rely on our faith. Like Abraham, our relationship to God becomes more established through faith, regardless of whether we are able to abide by all the commandments. The most celebrated men and women in the Bible violated the commandments. They were people who believed that God cared about them unconditionally, whether or not they sinned. Their remorse for transgressions demonstrated their desire to have and restore their relationship with God. These men and women viewed their relationship with God as valuable.

Like many days when I was a prison chaplain, I sat with a woman who had killed someone. As she spoke to me about her crime, the woman sobbed with remorse. I was able to see the depth of her anguish and her egret for her past behavior. Between sobs, she repeatedly said, "You do not know how bad I hurt, knowing what I have done." The woman kept asking me when I thought her hurt would subside. She questioned how she could continue to live with the memory of the crime she had committed. This woman remains in tremendous emotional pain over a killing that happened two years before. Any individual who watched her would realize that this woman had not gotten away with murder. Like most inmates with similar experiences, she most likely will not kill again, even in self-defense. The repercussions for this type of crime are enormous. This woman spoke in particular of how she re-lived her crime in flashbacks and nightmares that were triggered constantly. I often wonder if Moses and David knew a similar type of torment over having killed. Perhaps their sense of being forgiven contributed to their becoming moral leaders.

While these are extreme cases, the same experience can be true for all of us. That is, when we are generally aware of our sin, we can appreciate God's forgiveness, care, and love. I believe the language of Ten

Commandments plays an instrumental role in eliciting our dependency on God alone to forgive and restore us to relationship with God

Many scholars believe that the "thou shalt nots" originally referred to those commandments, that when broken, were punishable by the death penalty. "Thou shalt not kill" most likely referred to a prohibition against murder, which meant punishment by death. Adultery and stealing, both things and persons, also may have received the death penalty.

The idea conveyed in the Hebrew equivalent of "thou shalt not" is a total prohibition. This prohibition also appears in Genesis where it is a prohibition against eating from the tree of knowledge of good and evil. The total prohibition that is intended in the Hebrew version cannot be powerfully and succinctly captured in English. "Thou shalt not" in English has almost become a comically impotent phrase. For example, we may laugh about it while we poke fun at signs that prohibit trespassing or jaywalking. Jokingly, we say to one another, "thou shalt not." I conclude that the intent of the Ten Commandments is entirely too vast for us to cover in one small book. Its purposes that initially seem obvious are many and varied. Perhaps what we bring to the commandments says more about us than about the text itself.

One learning about the Ten Commandments that we could allow ourselves would be how to read them. Of course we could experiment with different ways to read them to maximize our experience. Obviously if we meditate on the commandments we will continue to gain in ways that we couldn't consciously expect, since meditation will produce different experiences depending on how we are feeling and thinking at the time.

Another method is letting the text speak to us from a semi-trance state by treating the text as sacred words to us. Doing so can alter how you experience the text. Allowing the text to be a set of directives to attain, to refrain, and to guide our lives could become a compassionate and protective experience. The Ten Commandments more than other texts seem to imply and invite that type of mental treatment.

Matthew

The Beatitudes are beautiful. A short chapter cannot give enough justice to the beauty, wisdom, and power contained in the life-altering words. Fortunately, I do not intend to do any such thing. Instead, I hope to simply call attention to some of the ways hypnotic power is used in these verses. When people change for the positive, it is delightful. When they seem to do it by gracefully surrendering their spirit to a more healthful way of living, it is remarkable.

When asked to describe in two words what she would like to change about herself, the average woman in prison would say, "My attitude." My training as a therapist did not prepare me to initially hear goals so abstract, broad, and easily mouthed with no apparent commitment. At first, I became angry that individuals took so little effort to think about their goals. As I have grown in wisdom, I now realize that an attitude change is exactly what was in order for these women. In a similar way, the Beatitudes can subtly change our attitude as we read them and take them into our psyches.

When we change our attitude, we are transforming the way in which we view the world, our future, our past, and ourselves. This encompasses most of what we need to change. An attitude change involves understanding life and self in a whole new way. The attitude change alters the entire universe. In fact, such a shift in perception may be all that we do when we make major changes.

I no longer attempted to get these women to state the "right" goal. I worked with them to understand their goals in ways that highlighted practical applications. What they were essentially changing, however, was their attitude. One beauty of the Beatitudes is the subtle way in which they alter our attitudes about God, life, and ourselves. There is real power in poetry that enters our soul in such a gentle and kind manner. I hope that I encourage people in a similar way to make helpful changes for themselves.

The hypnotic devices in these verses alter how we see the world and our place in that world. The words are used to alter readers' direction and attitude about the world, and themselves in the world. Although the text invites a humble attitude toward God's words, it also invites a change in perspective. Allowing yourself to be dwelling on how you see the world and accepting the text's view of the world certainly gives peace. For those persons blocked by their focus on themselves, this text invites a more outward focus. It also invites a more peaceful outlook about the world. To intentionally allow the words to alter how you view the world even for a short period of time is likely to provide some peaceful and calming effects. As you let the text invite you into a more comfortable place, this can help you get to that place of comfort with the text. Then the text can become a doorway into a peaceful place both now and in the future.

NRSV
Matthew 5:1-12
The Beatitudes

1 When Jesus saw the crowds, he went up the mountain; and after he sat down, his disciples came to him.	Paces and elicits expectancy. Frames the teaching.
2 Then he began to speak, and taught them saying:	Paces and elicits expectancy. Frames the teaching.
3 "Blessed are the poor in spirit, for theirs is the kingdom of heaven.	Indirect suggestion; reframe congratulates position; use of symbol; present tense.
4 "Blessed are those who mourn, for they will be comforted.	Reframe; symbol of inclusion; congratulates position; future orientation; tense.
5 "Blessed are the meek, for they will inherit the earth.	Indirect suggestion; reframe; future orientation,; symbol.
6 "Blessed are those who hunger and thirst for righteousness, for they will be filled.	Indirect suggestion; symbol; future orientation; reframe; directive.

7 "Blessed are the merciful, for they will receive mercy.	Indirect suggestion; reframe; future orientation.
8 "Blessed are the pure in heart, for they will see God.	Indirect suggestion; reframe; future orientation.
9 "Blessed are the peacemakers, for they will be called children of God.	Indirect suggestion; reframe; future orientation.
10 "Blessed are those who are persecuted for righteousness' sake, for theirs is the kingdom of heaven.	Reframe; symbol; ordeal; indirect suggestion; change to present tense.
11 "Blessed are you, when people revile you and persecute you and utter all kinds of evil against you falsely on my account.	Reframe; Symbol; indirect suggestion; process instructions.
12 Rejoice and be glad, for your reward is great in heaven, for in the same way they persecuted the prophets who were before you."	Reframe; symbol of success; process instructions; directive.

Because they set stage for Jesus' teaching, the first two verses are labeled as pacing. These verses help us to understand the similar context in which Jesus was teaching. The gospel author's use of escalation in Jesus' teaching style results in an air of expectancy for us. Verse 3 contains an indirect suggestion to be "poor in spirit" since this is the condition that is being blessed. The author's use of "poor in spirit" also marks a point of identification for most of us. Because the term is vague, it becomes a symbol toward which we can project our hopes. Given our interpretations of the verse's message, the writer's vagueness can allow us to feel confronted in helping the poor or the poor in spirit. The overall verse reframes the idea of being poor or poor in spirit. While the world's view of being poor is almost a curse, the author treats it as a state worthy of being blessed. As such, those of us who can identify with being poor in spirit are subtly congratulated on our position.

They shall be comforted" is a shift to future tense beginning in verse 4. The reward received is to be in the future. All other verses, with the exception of verse 10, remain in the future tense. While it is a subtle shift, this change has an effect on how we experience the following verses. If comfort were what we were supposed to feel while mourning, few people would initially identify with this verse. The fact that we can begin to feel comforted is a truth, however, that all can experience. When the writer originally wrote these words, this type of attention to detail was used to give the hearers and readers a positive experience.

We all aspire to become meek in order to receive the blessing promised to us in verse 5. Regardless of whether we label ourselves as meek, agreement with the writer subtly encourages us to become meek. This indirect suggestion to value being meek is powerful. The vagueness of meek as a symbol allows us to selectively examine ourselves. As readers, we declare ourselves meek according to our own definition.

The writer reframes the concept of meekness. While the world supposedly values aggressiveness, or at least assertiveness, this verse declares the opposite to be what God blesses. The overall orientation to this blessing continues to be in the future. Since it is easy for us to recognize that being meek is not immediately rewarded by the world, we cannot dispute the fact that this is a future blessing.

Everyone hungers and thirsts. Some of us even hunger and thirst for righteousness. No matter how minimal our efforts, we can all include ourselves in this category defined in verse 6. With this inclusion, however, we are committing ourselves to hunger and thirst even more. While the state of being righteous is not blessed in verse 6, the condition of hungering and thirsting after righteousness is. Those of us who are desiring righteousness and, perhaps, feeling aware of our sin are in the process of reframing ourselves. In fact, the more we are aware of our sin, the more likely we are to be hungering and thirsting after righteousness. The burden of sin and real remorse can cause us to deeply desire a cleansing and a righteousness that can only be described as hungering and thirsting. Even the cruelest person can declare him or herself merciful and hold the belief that this seventh verse also refers to himself or herself. I have met some of the meanest people, who claim that their behavior is merciful and kind. It is interesting that in simply reading these words and desiring for these attributes to be applicable to ourselves, we are also choosing to become more merciful. The term merciful is given high status here in contrast to the world's value of winning at all cost. This is the tool the author uses to reframe our existing idea of mercy. Future orientation continues in verse 7 as we recognize that the reward is declared for some future time.

At first thought, who of us can claim to be "pure in heart?" Verse 8 gives us a powerful indirect suggestion to be more pure in heart. The very state of knowing that we are not pure but desire to be so helps create in us a yearning for more purity. Except for those who are thinking pure thoughts, who among us does not want to see God? Since the writer is not referring to sin here, perhaps there is hope that we can achieve this state of purity. Most of us can choose to believe we are on our way. Even the most criminally minded person can overlook his/her sinful thoughts and dwell on the kind ones. In this way, he/she can realize that this type of purity is possible. It follows that people who desire to be "pure of heart" are also on their way, since their desires count as righteousness. Once again, the author reframes our experience of "pure in heart." The future is when we are promised to receive our reward.

Every co-dependent person realizes, if they are being honest, that verse 9 refers to them. Co-dependent individuals have spent their lives attempting to make peace in their households, and wherever else they have found themselves. Adding to this perspective, most people want to be peacemakers. Because many different types of peacemaking can be attributed to this vague meaning of peacemaking, the term itself is inclusive. This concept of pacification also serves to reframe the world's value that is placed on war making, winning, and conquering. The reward is again promised in the future.

It is not accidental that the author changes to present tense in verse 10. Instead of a reward to be pledged in the future, the time for compensation is now, "for theirs is the kingdom of heaven." This reframing of the experience is current. If we are being persecuted, we can now understand it as a blessing. Seeing our injustice as verification of being blessed is a powerful reframing. The art of using persecution as a symbol of our success is, in effect, turning the world's values and victimization upside-down.

Verse 11 is a continuation of the same theme and involves a similar reframe for coping with ill treatment. The writer indirectly suggests to us that ill treatment is symbolic of our prosperity. In other words, persecution is to be valued. During times of injustice, these words can be comforting. Unfortunately, this text does not include a disclaimer for the truly suspicious or the highly criminally minded. Both of these groups of people seem to misuse this interpretation as a license to ignore their behaviors. Hypnotic language simply does not address this type of distortion.

The gospel author continues the theme of reframing persecution in the final verse of this passage. Unlike the previous verses, there is a directive, "rejoice and be glad." Being persecuted is a symbol of our being like the prophets of old. Initially, most of us are unable to really move from a position of feeling hurt from injustices to a place of gladness. Perhaps we instead feel guilty that we are not able to feel grateful for our persecution. Usually once we become accustomed to being treated unfairly, we decide to move toward being glad. While initially we still do not like, for example, being someone else's target, we can also know that being joyful is a possibility. I experienced this type of persecution at the prison when inmates either lied or targeted me with their anger because I chose not to sanction a sin or rule violation in the institution. Because of the constant occurrences of these injustices, I have come to appreciate this verse in particular. While I did not master this process of rejoicing about persecution, the transition from feeling the injustice to stopping the pain no longer hurt as much.

The beauty and overall meaning of these verses is not really addressed through simply recognizing the described hypnotic devices. The whole is much more than the sum of its parts. The Beatitudes represent more than just the language devices that are employed in sentence structures. In addition to being a window on Jesus' teaching, the

Beatitudes are also a beautiful collection of wise sayings that we can use to direct our lives toward purpose and peace.

I want to change my attitude" is a common response I got when asking inmates what they wanted to change about themselves. Attitude, according to them, was the one thing that brought them to prison, caused them difficulty before prison, and remained to get in their way while in prison. For years I heard this culprit as an excuse, as an easy way to avoid identifying areas for improvement. When reframing it in light of the Beatitudes, however, I realized that perhaps it was a profound insight about how criminality reveals itself in our attitudes.

The "poor in spirit" are people who have conquered the ego in such a way that they no longer have a need for things to be all right. A need to steal is prompted by a belief that one is not enough simply as one is. This statement is true regardless of whether that perceived need is fueled by a drug addiction. Being poor in spirit, or humble, is an attitude that allows people the freedom to keep from breaking rules. It is only when people know that they have value, that they can become humble enough to obey laws. When people think they are worthless and use arrogance to cover their shame, then they are not going to care about obeying rules. People with incredibly low self-esteem usually are the ones who get into the most trouble.

The following story illustrates this idea of how improving self-esteem improves the way one behaves. A woman had committed vehicular manslaughter before laws existed to criminalize the act. When she came to prison, her line of offenses almost gave the appearance that she had demanded that the police lock her up. In prison, she managed to anger most of the inmates in one way or another. One weekend, she alienated almost everyone by visiting with another woman's husband. As a result of her behavior, she spent a lot of time in lockup while in prison. She eventually got into therapy and began to work on her past. She addressed the reasons why she felt so bad about herself, and how these feelings subsequently caused her to act out in negative ways. This woman honestly shared her nightmares and constant remorse that she carried for taking a woman's life while she was driving drunk. She knew that no amount of self-inflicted pain was going to make the incident better. She also realized that until she could forgive herself, the self-inflicted pain had somehow helped. Over time, this woman began to allow evidence of her remorse to be seen in daily actions that were respectful of life. By the time she left prison, she had a new "poor in spirit" attitude. In addition, this woman seemed to be mourning. She had definitely become meek and was seeking to be righteous. In fact, her kindness was borne out of her having received mercy and her desiring to give this forbearance to others. I am uncertain if she ever saw God, but I do know that some women observed God's forgiveness in her. She had truly changed her life and seemed to be grateful for having been forgiven.

In many respects, it is an attitude change that allows people with criminal behaviors to be transformed into caring and honest people. I have been fortunate enough to witness this miraculous change happen again and again. As some folks claim, these are the BE ATTITUDES, as opposed to the DON'T BE, and subsequently carry more power. In the 12-step tradition, people recognize that becoming clean and sober initially means changing their attitudes of pride while becoming humble enough to admit their need for help. It is an appropriate first step. Living with the spiritual knowledge that we are in need of grace and help can humble us. Knowing this is enough sometimes for us to qualify as the meek, or the poor in spirit. In any event, it is only when we can honestly acknowledge our poverty, that we can become rich spiritually.

Psalms

An inmate in cellblock once asked me, "Chaplain, why do I enjoy reading the psalms so much?" Her question both intrigued and haunted me. While I cannot explain her enjoyment of the psalms for certain, I do know of specific reasons that other people frequently read them. Throughout the ages, the psalms have meant a variety of things to different people. The texts have been sung in poetic songs and used as words of comfort, instruction, or vindication. The psalms have been a part of both public and private worship. Perhaps part of their global appeal can be attributed to the idea that as songs or poems, they can be understood specifically by what we bring to them. For example, our needs are usually met when we bring to the psalms our needs for uplifting and openness.

As poetry, and particularly through metaphors, the psalms can touch our deepest emotions and help us to feel understood, encouraged, and less lonely. At other times, they can serve as an outlet for anger, or a vindication for our feelings of being persecuted through attacks. This affirmation occurs regardless of whether we invite offenses. The psalms can also help us experience the joy of praise by validating our appreciation for what God has done for us.

Scholars have classified the psalms into linguistic types. Theologians and educators have scrutinized them with every possible tool. By carefully examining the psalms, translators have added to the beauty of the text by making them more readable for us. The countless hours of painstaking work involved in translating the Psalms accurately and faithfully enrich their meaning. This occurs if we, through our faith, treat the scholars' work, as God's caring for us. The faith of writers, translators, scholars, and readers throughout the ages is both humbling and inspiring. History still attests to the power found in the psalms.

Because of the variety of written perspectives on the psalms, scholars have yielded much knowledge and insight. By using historical criticism, incarnational criticism, form criticism and rhetorical criticism, scholars have discovered intuitiveness that can only be grasped through particular forms of thought. Because each vantage point highlights a specific examination of the psalms, each type of criticism illuminates the text differently and brings us new understandings.

We are all indebted to the people who have spent their lifetimes apprehending, translating, and reviewing the psalms through critical methods. Their work results in great insight and understanding for us about ourselves. We can also gain an appreciation for the psalms as a unique part of scripture. Any brief recitation of the wealth of information discovered by others would not be respectful enough to any of the schools of thought represented. I can only hope that my admiration for these scholars and their work and faith is communicated, in part by my refraining from describing their work with either the psalms or other biblical texts.

The psalms can also be understood through the unique linguistic framework of hypnosis. It is my intent to show that this is possible through examination of one type of psalm in each broad category described by A.B. Rhodes, Ph.D. 1) Hymns of Praise, 2) Prayers in Times of Trouble, 3) Affirmations of Faith, 4) Songs of Thanksgiving, 5) Wisdom Poetry, 6) Liturgies, and 7) Mixed Poems (which either shows a free composition or is an adaptation of earlier materials).

Psalm 100 is the most familiar of the type categorized as a Hymn of Praise. The New Interpreters Bible states the following about Psalm 100: "In a sense, psalm 100 demonstrates the typical structure of a song of praise: invitation for praise (vv. 1-4), followed by reasons for praise (v.5)."

Praise literature invites us into a mindset of praise. In this psalm it is invited through direct commands in the verses. When we are willing to go along with the commands and praise God, we are likely to experience the uplifting of spirit, and we can be appreciative to God. Think about it. God commands us to praise God and we get blessed. We can also recognize that it was built in for us in the scriptures. Being willing to enter a mindset of praise is quite different than the one generated by Philippians, Matthew, or the Ten Commandments. Yet, being willing to enter a state of mind that is praising God is going to have an effect on how we feel about ourselves, as well as how we feel about God. While praise might indirectly impact how we experience the world, the direct focus is chiefly on impacting our emotions and on how we view God. I believe that it is no accident that the one brings about the other.

NRSV
Psalm 100
A Psalm of Thanksgiving

1 Make a joyful noise to the Lord, all the earth.	Implied command; implicit positive relationship; expectation and certainty.
2 Worship the Lord with gladness; come into his presence with singing.	Implied command; instruction; second command; wisdom expectation; certainty.
3 Know that the Lord is God. It is he that made us, and we are his, we are his people, and the sheep of his pasture.	Implied command; instruction; implicit world view; relationship between reader and God.
4 Enter his gates with thanksgiving, and his courts with praise. Give thanks to him, bless his name.	Implied command; wisdom; Second and Third commands; implied relationship of thankfulness.
5 For the Lord is good; his steadfast love endures forever, and his faithfulness to all generations.	Implied message that God is worthy, that we owe him, that we can count on God's being there for us, and that we can feel secure.

In the first verse, we are given a command to make a joyful noise. That the writer has the right to command the reader is implied. The author implicitly dictates both to the reader and himself to make joyful noise. Compliance is presumed while joy is treated as a state of mind rather than an emotion. If we look at joyful noise literally, the writer implies that our emotion does not affect the type of noise we are

directed to make. Yet, the noise is to be joyful. It is common knowledge that music can be joyful, sorrowful, peaceful, or angry.

Does the author intend to imply that we are to be joyful, or to make
joyful noise? From a hypnotic standpoint, I think the answer is yes to
all of the above. The answer that we find to be most meaningful is the
correct one. Trance logic is literal. From a trance state, we hear and
respond with a concrete mindset. And it is our particular mindset and
expectation that become shaped. Whether we bring a willingness to
make a joyful noise, a desire to make noise joyfully, or an ability to
make a joyful noise joyfully, our mindset resides within us.

We are instructed and commanded to make a joyful noise to the
Lord. The author also teaches us to address the Lord with joy. When
we address the Lord in this manner, we are putting ourselves into a
mental state where we can experience the Lord in a particular way.
This is different from speaking to the Lord with compliance, anger, or
arrogance. By using this comparison, we can see that there is a genuine
difference between an attitude that is joyful and one that is needy and
demanding.

There is deep wisdom when we speak to the Lord from a joyful
place. The world and our relationship with God appear differently
than from a place of sorrow or hopelessness. If we address it in this
way, it is much more likely that we will also become joyful. We will
most certainly experience God as speaking to us from joy. Viewing the
world through a window of suspicion makes everything look suspicious. Depending on which lens of emotion we choose to see the world
through, our surroundings will appear differently and we will receive a
variety of answers and conclusions.

Everyone and everything is commanded to make a joyful noise.
What a wonderful way to understand the pandemonium of the
world—joyful noise to the Lord, made by the world. If we interpreted
the clamor in our lives as being joyfully made to the Lord, perhaps it
would change our experience of the noise, from an irritating state to
one of celebration. In this verse, we find an implicit expectancy of

compliance. This decisiveness, or flavor of certainty, is alone hypnotic. When we become entirely convinced of our thoughts, and enthusiastically proclaim them to others, our hearers have a natural tendency to adopt our spirited beliefs. Certainty has a way of capturing doubt and leading it to a new destination.

In the second verse, we are again directed, and also instructed, on how to worship God. Specifically, we are to worship God with gladness. To be in a state of gladness or thankfulness is at the heart of worship. Worshiping from this place allows us to become both appreciative and happy. We are commanded to worship with gladness and to "come into his presence with singing." This implicit command charges us to knowingly approach the Lord's presence. Even though the Lord is ultimately everywhere, we are still commanded to come into God's presence. Doing this requires us to be aware and to intentionally seek the Lord.

Complaining is the opposite of worshiping. By using complaints, we are implying that we have all of the answers. We are, in effect, declaring that we are the higher authority that can judge God's actions. In a state of grumbling, our complaints rarely serve to make us feel better. Whining about how God treats us is indirectly saying that God does not care or is incapable of knowing us or doing something for us. Parents and children alike can become resentful for the same reasons. Grumbling between a parent and a child rarely endears one to the other. Complaints implicitly comment on the relationship, sending an implied message that is negative and judging.

In this second verse we are also given a message to approach the Lord with singing. Singing can certainly break our everyday trances of living and simply going through the motions. Regardless of whether we can sing well, we are more likely to feel different emotionally than if we choose not to sing. Even singing the blues is a way of becoming happier. Perspective changes through singing. We attempt to reconcile ourselves to a rhythm, and to adjust our tone to a prescribed musical tone. This occurs when we are willingly, rather than grudgingly, able to adapt our voices. We can even joyfully do this adjustment when we find we are in harmony with our neighbors. There is deep wisdom in what singing communicates to us about how to worship.

We worship with gladness, not sadness, seriousness, or correctness. Revering God in this particular way encourages us to like ourselves, too. It also invites us to enjoy the act of worshiping. Worship is an intimate time between God and us. This intimacy is best developed when we enter into worship away from our everyday routines and with gladness. The command in the second verse is given with the same certainty and expectation as in the first verse. The statement carries the same type of power to motivate us.

In verse 3, the command is not stated with the same strength as in previous verses. It reads with more hope, or desire, for the reader to "know that the Lord is God." Even the remainder of the writer's declaration that "it is he that made us" reads with more of a flavor of faith than of certainty. Yet it is this change in tone that allows us to form a relationship based on willingness rather than on commands. Implicitly stated here is the truth that we are the created and not the creator. We are to be obedient to God and not commanding. It is interesting that rather than directing, the author instead states this to us through the breath of faith. As such, this style of writing evokes an invitation for us to understand God and ourselves in a connected and intimate relationship as sheep are to their shepherd. We are invited to be proud of belonging, and this even further defines the relationship between God and ourselves, and even the writer and God. It is written with a reverence, not a command. We are the sheep of his pasture. Indirectly stated is that THE SHEPHERD will be our protector and provider. The Shepherd's continuous presence and care are implicit.

Verse four says, "Enter his gates with thanksgiving, and his courts with praise. Give thanks to him, bless his name." To enter God's gates and courts is our directive. We are also told to give thanks and bless his name. Our desire is not in question, so our compliance is presumed. Implicit in this presupposition is the notion that the writer has the right to command us. In addition, it is assumed that we have things to be grateful for and the capacity to be thankful. When we operate from this presumed position, the world appears differently. We begin to focus on our gratitude in other areas and we begin to evoke a grateful attitude, which changes our emotions and whatever else we perceive.

The writer's statement is more difficult to disagree with when we presumably have praise and thanksgiving. This is because it is assumed rather than directly stated. It follows that we implicitly accept more of these assumptions, if the author's statement goes unchallenged. The more we accept a worldview without questioning it, the more we incorporate that particular viewpoint as our own.

Also contained within the command to give thanks and praise is a subtler piece of wisdom. This is an implication of our ability to enter God's gates and courts. We enter into the Lord's presence through our usage of praise and thanksgiving. Rather than being a requirement, praise and thanksgiving symbolize a gate, a key, or a ticket. When we are thankful, we enter into a state of mind where we become ready to encounter the Lord. We are much more likely to experience God as nurturing and loving when we are in an open state of happiness, joy, or spontaneous appreciation. Our desire to be obedient to God also stems from these feelings of gratitude and praise.

The final verse says, "For the Lord is good; his steadfast love endures forever, and his faithfulness to all generations." This verse implies that God is worthy. The previous verses referred to our thankfulness, while this contrasting one speaks about God's worthiness. This verse also indirectly states that we owe a debt to God for his enduring love and faithfulness and that we can feel secure because of this fact. Since these ideas are not directly stated, we are much more likely to accept them without question. Furthermore, people who desire to scrutinize the words of this psalm most certainly want to learn about God and become closer to God.

In discovering that the psalm has implied statements that are positive, we can grin and appreciate that these messages have been placed there for us to discover. If this psalm is examined closely, we will realize that it is a hidden love letter to us to be discovered.

At a first glance, Psalm 100 appears to be a light passage that can be used to comment on our nervousness about singing. In addition, we may declare that we are making a joyful noise. This psalm is also gives us a straightforward message about praising God. While on the surface it may look like a joyful psalm without much substance, further study reveals the instructional value it has for us. This passage conveys much of the characteristic theology of the psalms while it invites us to experience a more powerful relationship with God.

Obviously, this psalm employs hypnotic tools for conveying messages in powerful ways. Are some of these tools used in ordinary poetry? The obvious answer is yes. Hypnotic language is intentional with its use of what is conveyed. This applies to what is written both in and between the lines of the text. A hypnotist always uses the same language tools that can be found in good poetry.

Prayer in Time of Trouble

Psalm 12 is a prayer in time of trouble. It can be read as a prayer for either an individual or a group. In addition to its beauty, this particular psalm concisely demonstrates the phenomenon of hypnotic language used in the psalms.

Prayers in times of trouble capture the feeling of being alone while facing adversity. The feelings then change to include our relationship to God. It is as if the psalm invites identification and then uses that emotion to offer a new perspective about our situation and about God. In general, no matter how you come to this passage it is uplifting and affirming. No wonder these psalms are used so frequently by people to assist themselves and others in times of trouble.

NRSV
PSALM 12: 1-8,
I Will Now Arise

1 Help, O Lord, for there is no longer anyone who is godly; the faithful have disappeared from humankind.	Establishes rapport; paces, and creates emotional drama; indirect compliment
2 They utter lies to each other; with flattering lips and a double heart they speak.	Continuation of drama; more pacing; indirect positive regard; reframe and congratulation. Subtle change of position.
3 May the Lord cut off all flattering lips, the tongue that makes great boasts, subtle reframe of readers'	Elicits expectancy; continued rapport; begins move to main intervention; position of righteousness; indirect compliment; and beginning of experience reframe
4 those who say, "With our tongues we will prevail; our lips are our own-who is our master?"	Interspersal; confusion indirect wisdom; indirect confrontation; and reframe.
5 "Because the poor are despoiled, because the needy groan, I will now rise up," says the LORD; "I will place them in the safety for which they long."	Fantasy rehearsal; inter-spersal; confusion; indirect reassurance; and affirmation of God and relationship between reader and God.
6 The promises of the LORD are promises that are pure, silver refined in a furnace on the ground, purified seven times.	Symbolized problem is changed; indirect self-affirmation; reframe of situation.
7 You, O LORD, will protect us; you will guard us from this generation forever.	Indirect comfort; personalized relationship.
8 On every side the wicked prowl, as vileness is exalted among humankind.	Changes ratified; amnesia.

In the first verse, rapport is being built using the emotional identification between us, as readers, and the writer. Most likely, we can identify with the author by feeling alone and betrayed, or isolated in a world of corruption. We are subtly invited to become the writer through identification. Even if we are not presently feeling unique in our striving to be faithful or less lonely, perhaps we can remember a time when we felt that way. Thus an emotional drama is being developed. God is spoken to directly. At the same time, we are indirectly affirmed as faithful, regardless of whether we are. There is "no longer anyone who is godly." Even if we do not experience feelings of faithfulness, this compliment is more difficult to dispel because it is implied. This is especially true given that the focus of this verse is that "the faithful have disappeared."

"Help, O Lord for there is no longer anyone who is godly." Is this attitude not typical of us? We continually reach out to God for help only when we have exhausted our supply of supportive people. The writer is admitting to putting God last in his/her life. It is unfortunate that we often wait until the last moment to request God's help. Yet this psalm seems to accept this attitude while endorsing the author, who has vicariously admitted that he/she shares this dilemma.

The phrase "the faithful have disappeared from humankind" comments on the state of the writer. He/she is unable to see people who are faithful. Perhaps the author has been unfaithful and/or has had others treat him/her with disdain for shameful acts that have been committed. Maybe the writer is truly righteous and is only stating how unfaithful others have been to him/her. The fact remains that the author feels like he/she is alone in dealing with unfaithful ones. If we are to interpret the psalm intellectually, we may conclude that the writer and/or the reader are engaging in projection. Yet if the psalm is understood from the concrete nature of a trance state, then we, alone, are striving to be faithful. We also need help, and are aware of the sinful nature of those around us.

In verse 2, the drama continues. Others are against the writer, and thus against us. Through the identification of being lied against and lied to, there is also more pacing of the emotion. The lies of others are also identified. When we are dishonest, even in the small ways referred to as white lies, then part of what becomes impaired is our ability to trust. The more that we lie, the more our ability to trust becomes impaired. When we are dishonest with ourselves, we cannot trust others. Therefore, in order to participate in the drama, we must be in denial. It follows that we convince ourselves that others are lying while we are the only ones left who are telling the truth.

Again, it is not important if we are fooled either by our own deception or by being naive. If we find ourselves feeling that others have lied to us and that because of our belief we cannot trust others, we are continuing the drama. Who among us has not been the target of others' lies at one time or another. This feeling can originate either from us or from the actual behavior of others. Regardless of whether or not others are lying, the feelings that we experience from our beliefs remain the same.

In verse 3, we are building expectancy by shifting to what we want God to do. Since it is the natural progression of this psalm, we are continuing rapport. Yet ever so subtly, our position of righteousness is beginning to be reframed. The writer's words of hope that "the Lord cut off all flattering lips," are exclusive. Indirectly, the author is reaffirmed as being righteous, in contrast to those whose lips are flattering. We can identify, however, with either the people with flattering lips or the righteous writer. In either case, the psalm speaks indirectly to us. The writer embodies the capacity to both flatter and desire righteousness. The inner conflict over the author's dishonesty is beginning to be addressed. As readers, our inner conflict about honesty is also highlighted. Who among us has not refrained from getting into trouble by exaggerating even in small ways. Even if today we are committed to the truth, we still struggle to verify our own honesty. All of us at one time or another have used flattery while being less than completely honest with others.

Verse 4 has some interesting twists and turns such as "those who say, 'With our tongues we will prevail; our lips are our own—who is our master?'" On one level, this verse is the continuation of verse 3, and at another it is saying something quite different. First, the words are continuing the description of those with flattering lips. Yet on another level, we are the ones being described. At yet another level the writer is saying that "with our tongues we will prevail." Again we have an inner conflict coupled with a hidden message that WE WILL PRE-VAIL. It is with our tongue that we both pray and prevail. Within this message is also the condemnation of a particular attitude of self. The conflicting messages are contained in this verse. When did conflicting, seemingly contradictory statements change the truth? Inside of us we hold both truths, and we can address these at the same time in one sentence. When we agree with the condemnation of some action, we are also endorsing the fact that we will stop or attempt to end an action. Even if we are only reinforcing our agreement, we are giving ourselves notice by our consent. Regardless of how self-righteous or righteous we might profess to be in our condemnation, we are speaking directly to ourselves.

The main intervention begins in verse 5. On the behalf of the poor, "I will now rise up." Fantasy rehearsal elements are found in this verse. Often we can give ourselves permission to rise up, or come to our senses for someone else, even if we cannot do this for ourselves. Interspersal technique can be noted here as the writer and reader state the words, "I will now rise up." The next line takes us back to the original plea, continuing the interspersal technique. "I will place them in the safety for which they long." The writer originally asks for help, while he/she longs for safety. There is an indirect reassurance found on two levels. The first reassurance is accomplished with interspersal and the second is that God will place them in safety. "Them" refers to both the reader and the writer. While there is an affirmation of God and God's willingness to help, there is also an implied positive relationship between the writer and God, and the reader and God. This is due to the fact that the writer has written it in such a way that we can identify with the writer.

The second part of the main intervention is in verse 6. The author again speaks on multiple levels. On one level, this verse is an affirmation of God's promises. On another level, the symbol of the writer's original problem is being changed. The author has been going through the process of being refined in a furnace and purified by trial. With

God's intervention, both the writer and us, as readers, are now able to feel good about ourselves. The writer's initial situation changes. Feeling both afraid and alone has become a purifying process that affirms God's partnership. We, like the writer, are no longer alone. The psalm has reframed the original situation.

Simultaneously, verse 7 affirms God and what God intends to do. That is, protect us and guard us. It is also indirectly affirming to the reader/writer. We are affirmed because the relationship is more personal and comforting than it was in verse 1. That God will protect us also indirectly asserts that God cares about us and that we are important to God. The feelings of being hurt, fearful, and alone found in verse 1 have been replaced with feelings of security, affirmation, and intimacy. Notice also how the implied aloneness of verse 1 is altered by the use of the word "us." "The Lord will protect us." The reader and the writer are no longer alone.

This psalm has done its work. Now we are less likely to feel alone, afraid, or persecuted. If we have identified with the writer in thinking that he/she was uniquely righteous, then the affirmation of God's care implied here indicates that our sin has been forgiven. This transformation occurs even though the writer never speaks directly about forgiveness. Because both the sin and the forgiveness are implied, an implicit confession and cleansing forgiveness are the results. In some ways, this is more powerful than if forgiveness had been the stated topic. It is not easy to feel forgiven if the forgiveness is spoken directly. Our feelings of unworthiness block us from our own willingness to receive release from our guilt. When forgiveness is implied, our typical habit of discounting, ignoring, resisting, or disbelieving does not work. Perhaps we will not consciously realize this fact but will simply feel better. Being asked directly if we feel forgiven tends to evoke feelings of aloneness and despair. The reason is that the question itself implies that our forgiveness is uncertain. Without the question, it is simple; we are forgiven.

The multiple levels of communication, inferred confessions, and forgiving statements found in the psalms clearly show some of the reasons why both prison inmates and the rest of us favor the psalms.

Verse 8 serves to ratify the changes for us that we have experienced, by completing a circle of information that began in verse 1. The writer again comments on the vileness and prowling nature of humankind. While different words are used to express the same idea as in verse1, we are now at a completely different place. The writer returns to the original idea while altering both the tone of the psalm and our relationship to God. Since this is done without discussion, we probably will not examine or stick with the changes. By ignoring these changes, the writer promotes amnesia for emotional and spiritual healing. The changes, in this case, are likely to continue.

Changing the subject, or promoting amnesia of some positive, implanted idea is much like placing a small amount of dirt over a seed. In the same way that the seed has been planted to grow, the idea has been sown, and will impact future self-calculations once accepted truth. Most likely we will observe this implantation in subtle ways. Perhaps we find ourselves more willing to use the Bible for comfort. We may also feel less guilt and sinfulness. It is probable that we will want to keep that feeling of closeness to God.

I am reminded of what an old preacher wrote in a Bible he was giving to a young person: "Either your sins will keep you from this Book, or this Book will keep you from your sins." Spontaneous trances occur while we are doing things other than reading the Bible. Common times include driving a car or engaging in some routine activity. When these trances occur while we are being self-depreciating, then our hurt, idolatry, and dysfunction becomes reinforced. For example, when we read the Bible while feeling depressed and self-effacing, it is possible for us to screen out passages that are healing while noticing only texts that promote self-criticism. When we are self-effacing, then we are implying that we do not deserve help, even from God. On the other hand, reading the Bible at times when we are hurting and needing comfort is implicitly self-affirming since we are giving ourselves the right to receive comfort from God. In a self-affirming trance, we are more likely to notice affirming passages that lead to our healing.

NRSV
PSALM 23
A Psalm of David

1 The Lord is my shepherd, I shall not want.	Establishes rapport; minimal Steps; elicits expectancy; Command; relational.
2 He makes me lie down in green pastures; he leads me beside still waters;	Command of permission; symbol used; drama begins; rapport; affirmation; and expectancy.
3 he restores my soul. He leads me in right paths for his name's sake.	Affirmation; implied positive; implied nurturing and care; and implied command to do good.
4 Even though I walk through the darkest valley, I fear no evil; for you are with me; your rod and your staff—they comfort me.	Pacing metaphor that implies care; interspersal; implied personal and positive relationship.
5 You prepare a table before me in the presence of my enemies; you anoint my head with oil; my cup overflows.	Time distortion; ambiguity; positive future orientation; and positive perspective.
6 Surely goodness and mercy shall follow me all the days my life, and I shall dwell in the house of the Lord my whole life long.	Positive future orientation; reframe of v. 4; commitment of invited and declared; changes ratified; direct and indirect suggestions.

Verse 1 establishes a rapport and begins moving us in small steps. "The Lord is my shepherd" is a declarative statement. It defines the relationship between us, the writer, and God. "The Lord is my shepherd" is set in the present. This line precedes "I shall not want," which is future-oriented. Since "the Lord is my shepherd" is ambiguous, we can understand it as meaning any one of four different interpretations. "I shall not want," can be understood as a future demand on ourselves: Since the Lord is our shepherd, we will not allow ourselves to want. It can also be interpreted as a realization that we will no longer be distracted by wants because the Lord will take good care of us. The declaration, "I shall not want" also contains a nurturing meaning. If we accept that the Lord totally takes care of us, then we let go of our will. Finally, this phrase can be understood as I shall not want another shepherd. In a sense, "I shall not want" encompasses all of the above meanings, and more. The ambiguity is one of the reasons many of us can identify with and gain from both reading and hearing this passage. It can used to mean what we need it to mean at any given time, provided it is in line with the other scriptures. This is part of the beauty, wisdom, and living relevance of the biblical texts. This particular passage is one that helps keep the scriptures alive for us whenever we choose to approach them.

Verse 2, "He makes me lie down in green pastures," is both a permissive statement for receiving comfort and a subtle command to lie down, to relax, to stop, and to enjoy what the Lord is giving. The same effect, with a slight difference, is found in the second part of the verse, "he leads me beside still waters." The symbols of green pastures and still waters combine the invitations for us to receive the calm, experience the peace, and be reminded that God is with us. An expectation of green pastures and still waters can either evoke the future, affirm the past, or acknowledge the present. Depending on how it is read, all three can apply. Because of its ambiguity, this verse continues to build rapport.

Verse 3 is also affirming. "He restores my soul," implies an acknowledgment that we have lost our way and that God has restored us to sound mind, senses, or self. At the same time, this phrase attests that God restores our souls in the future and in the present. The ambiguity of the tense allows any time frame to be envisioned by us, depending on our particular needs or beliefs.

There is implied nurturing and care in both the restoration of our souls and in the being led into right paths. Also implicit is the subtle directive to journey down right paths. The implicit danger of losing our soul is connected with not going down right paths. At the same time, this directive is not a command but a leading. We can experience it primarily as a caring encouragement to be safe. In referring to leading and paths, this verse sets the stage for the next verse, where an important intervention takes place.

The last phrase in verse 3, "for his name's sake," serves to remove the pressure from us. If it had been written for our sake, the author would have implied a duty or obligation. In this case, "for his name's sake" frees us so that we can receive. Most of us resent being taken hostage by another person's good deed that removes our freedom and enslaves us to do their bidding. Being indebted to someone can be a vulnerable position where we feel guilty and manipulated. This is especially true when it means giving up something we wanted. By disavowing the intent that generates this type of obligation, verse 3 invites us to appreciate what is done for us rather than resent a debt.

In verse 4, an important and yet subtle shift takes place. Up to this point, God has been referred to in the third person. God is now directly spoken to. As readers, we have, in effect, moved closer to God. This subtle transition also invites us to experience God as more personal as we continue our movement. The metaphor of the darkest valley, or the "valley of the shadow of death," is broad enough to encompass almost any crises to be projected and addressed. Whether our junctures are real or imagined, we can receive comfort from these words. Because of the universal character of this inclusiveness, most of us can identify with the metaphor. This is an example of sophisticated pacing.

I will fear no evil" are the next words after the universal pacing. While reading this text and repeating the words to ourselves, we are affirming our commitment to fear no evil. At the same time, we are directing ourselves to fear no evil. The writer also implies here that we will no longer need to be afraid since the Lord will be with us—"you are with me." The command is interspersed in the sentence and connected to this phrase. Similar to verse 1, "I will fear no evil" can be understood as a nurturing affirmation that God is with us.

The phrase "your rod and staff they comfort me" moves us back to verifying and ratifying our change of perception to the future. Those times when we have experienced God's correction, or nurturing, are in fact affirming time when God is with us. We all receive redirection from one source or another. If we view correction as God's rod, it becomes a comforting, implied suggestion for us. Our experience of God's comfort can also be deepened if we adopt this viewpoint, rather than resent being rectified.

"You prepare a table before me" begins a time ambiguity. We can interpret this passage as something God performed last week, is currently doing, or will be doing next month. Ambiguity allows all three perceptions to be correct. When we match it to our experience, it can be labeled as pacing, yet it can also set the tone for how we interpret difficult times when people seem to be against us. The words used by the so-called people against us can be reinterpreted in a positive way. This phrase begins to prepare us for the next two lines of affirmation.

Because "you anoint my head with oil, my cup overflows," is connected to enemies, it further frames the experience of having adversaries. The author states that God anoints our head with oil even though, because of, or in reaction to our enemies. Being anointed is a wonderful metaphor that allows for us to engage in all sorts of projection. This can be understood as a blessing, an announcement of special recognition, a commission, or an ordination to some further task, or role. This phrase's ambiguity is both affirming and inclusive.

A similar equivoque is evident in the statement, "my cup overflows." All sorts of meanings that affirm and match our experience can be ascribed to this phrase. In addition, the writer shows us a way to observe life. Regardless of how much or how little we see our cup as overflowing; it is a state of mind. This perspective is more than viewing the cup as half full or half empty. It is a way of observing ourselves as being blessed with our cup overflowing. This phrase is also an affirmation of how well we will be taken care of by God and are being taken care of by God.

Verse 6 simultaneously establishes a future orientation while reframing the "darkest valley" referred to in verse 4. In addition, this verse also proclaims a commitment and offers us both direct and indirect suggestions. Here the writer has packed a tremendous amount in less than 30 words of text.

In the surface structure of the following sentence, future orientation is evident. "Goodness and mercy shall follow me, and I shall dwell in the house" are both predicting and affirming the future. The positive goodness and mercy are in contrast to the darkest valley mentioned in verse 4. As such, the message that God will provide goodness and mercy overshadows the darkest valley. It gives us hope while altering how we experience the valley.

The phrase "surely goodness and mercy shall follow me all the days of my life," invites us to experience more mercy and goodness. This future affirmation subtly encourages us to feel calm nurturing through the implied mercy and affirmation. It also prepares us to verbalize the commitment found in the phrase "and I shall dwell in the house of the Lord all of my life." This commitment is both an indirect command for us to stay in the house of the Lord and a direct obligation to dwell in the house of the Lord. Since it is an interspersal technique that is tied to accepting the mercy and goodness, it is indirect. For example, if we accept goodness and mercy, then we are much more likely to accept the commitment. The obligation is placed in our mouth by the writer. The commitment is also stated as an overt experience hoped for in the future.

It is no small wonder that Psalm 23 receives so much acclaim. It contains numerous blessings for us. The brilliance of how the writer constructed this psalm is amazing. It uplifts us, while offering comfort, instruction, and guidance. When we realize the complexity of this psalm, we can continue to marvel at its effectiveness when it is approached with faith.

When the psalm is examined in various translations, it consistently reveals the same message. The hypnotic aspects of the psalm are translated in all of the various English versions. Some use more poetic language, and others use more ambiguity or less ambiguity. Regardless of style, all contain the same powerful effect. For people who have learned to love Psalm 23 in the King James Version, it is different because of the beloved and friendly nature of the familiar words. The known and appreciated words, however, have separate meaning from the text because of the translation, and because of our particular associations with the words. Like old friends, these familiar words that have brought comfort to us in the past are continually associated with this comfort. It is our associated comfort with a particular version, rather than with the words themselves, that gives us our feelings. Logic does not come into play when we consider the reasons we may feel more comfortable with a particular translation. Instead, it is our emotional baggage that we bring to the text that allows us to make an emotional connection.

Here are some examples of positive connections with Psalm 23 in the King James Version. An adult who memorized the psalm as a child with his/her grandmother remembers the feeling of accomplishment and praise his/her grandmother gave. Today, this person may carry a strong positive connection to the King James Version of Psalm 23. Another example might include someone who used the psalm in a tragic time. This individual may have connected to the comfort that he/she experienced during the time of loss or transition. Because of the traumatic nature of the loss, events may have become etched into his/her brain, and associated with the language of the King James Version. In a similar fashion, the denomination of a Christian tends to dictate which version is more appreciated because accepted. Catholics, Methodists, Presbyterians, Episcopalians, Pentecostals, and Evangelicals have their own accepted texts. Church groups tend to adopt one version, and those people who belong tend to conform. Not having or using the accepted text is not a sin; it simply is not as accepted as the standard text. Also, particular psalms tend to distinguish churches into groups in the same way as particular texts. Appreciating Psalm 23 is much more of a culturally Christian occurrence than a Jewish or Islamic one.

NRSV
Psalm 67
A Psalm of Thanksgiving
A Psalm. A Song

1 May God be gracious to us and bless us and make his face to shine upon us, {Selah}	Rapport building; indirect compliments; implied praise and value.
2 that your way may be known upon earth, your saving power among all nations.	Implicit positive relationship; indirect praise of reader.
3 Let the peoples praise you, O God; let all the peoples praise you.	Implied compliment, Indirect suggestion.
4 Let the nations be glad and sing for joy, for you judge the peoples with equity and guide the nations upon the earth. {Selah}	Indirect suggestion, Implicit care and concern. Implicit compliment.
5 Let the peoples praise you, O God; let all the peoples praise you.	Repeat of verse 3, yet intensified because of the repetition.
6 The earth has yielded its increase; God, our God, has blessed us.	Reframe of the earth; Implicit current blessing.
7 May God continue to bless us; let all the ends of the earth revere him.	Implicit current blessing; Implicit message that reverence of God is good.

Verse 1 is reminiscent of the traditional Jewish blessing often said by priests over their congregations. Compare it to the following passage from Numbers 6:22-27:

The Lord said to Moses, saying: Speak to Aaron and his sons, saying, Thus, you shall bless the Israelites: You shall say to them, The Lord bless you and keep you; the Lord make his face to shine upon you, and be gracious to you; the Lord lift up his countenance upon you, and give you peace. So they shall put my name on the Israelites, and I will bless them."

The sons of Aaron would most likely note that there is an implied compliment given to us by our simply being able to say the blessing. This is because this rabbinical blessing is appointed for priests only. Hence, when we read these words, we are invited to say the blessing also. The similarity of these two passages is in the message of being blessed. Because of its likeness to the Numbers passage, Psalms 67 also contains a rapport-building effect. The psalm writer's use of familiar words, ideas, and places can create an implicit acceptance for us with ourselves and those with common backgrounds. Using the familiar in order to develop rapport is an excellent method of employing an implied compliment while at the same time increasing effectiveness.

This verse contains another indirect compliment for us. Implied is the message that we, as readers, are already being treated as if we deserved to be blessed. Praising God is also suggested. In fact, while glorifying God, the entire psalm lifts us up. This is one of the ironic blessings that we can receive from praising God. Glorifying God results in also being lifted up. The effect is, in part, due to the indirect compliment. If our God is so great, then in some small measure, we, too, are OK. Yet, it is more than identification. This effect also relates to our guilt, self-esteem, faith, and relationship with God. The more we commend God, the more abundantly we receive.

Implied in the verse 2 of the psalm is our positive relationship with God. God is spoken to directly and with endearment instead of abstractly. This suggestion is found in the subtle shift from "May God" in the first verse to "your way" in the second. The writer's desire for us to know God points to a positive relationship. Further defined, this affirmative relationship highlights the following idea: If we love God, and express our closeness to God, then we are also acting as if we believe that God loves us.

In verse 3, the writer requests that God allow all the earth to praise God and asserts that it is a privilege to praise God. We are indirectly encouraged to praise God in two ways. The first way involves all the earth. Secondly, we are to interpret the writer's positive relationship to God as our experience while saying, reading, or hearing this text.

We are encouraged indirectly to praise God, be glad, and sing in verse 4. It also implies that God cares about the nations and desires good for them. By referring to God's "judging with equity," indirect assurance is given to us that God will deal with us fairly. We are also given a invitation to follow suit.

Verse 5 echoes verse 3. Since the same messages are repeated, similar implied messages occur. By repeating the verse, the emphasis is both increased and decreased. Hence, we pay more attention to the theme by reiterating it, and at the same time, tend to avoid concentrating on the message. With enough repetition, we are lulled into becoming distracted from implied messages, while at the same time focusing more on them. Both statements are true.

Because of its reference to the earth yielding its increase, some commentators believe that this particular verse was designed for use during a harvest time. Today, it functions as a part of everyday scriptures. We can read it daily and understand it in two different ways. "The earth has yielded its increase" is a particular way of thinking about the earth. While we occasionally only see the wait, or the work to be done, the earth has always yielded its increase. Affirming this particular viewpoint reframes the manner in which we traditionally think of the earth as providing only at harvest time. "God, our God, has blessed us" is a direct affirmation. At the same time, this statement implies that when the earth yields its increase, we are blessed by God. With an acknowledgment that the earth is perpetually yielding its increase comes an implied understanding that we are also being blessed during this time.

The final verse reaffirms this current blessing with an indirect suggestion that we, as readers, are currently being blessed. The word "continue" indicates that God is blessing us now. This verse also contains an implicit message that reverence for God is good. The act of desiring all the earth to honor God implies that we are blessed simply by choosing to have reverence for God. In other words, the act of revering God brings with it an inherent blessing.

NRSV
PSALM 15
A Psalm of David

1 O Lord, who may abide in your tent? Who may dwell on your holy hill?	Implied positive relationship to God; pacing; implied desire; element of drama.
2 Those who walk blamelessly, and do what is right, and speak the truth from their heart;	Indirect instruction; implied care for us; implied righteousness; and motivation.
3 who do not slander with their tongue, and do no evil to their friends, nor take up a reproach against their neighbors;	Simultaneous affirmation and confrontation; invitation to commitment; directive.
4 in whose eyes the wicked are despised, but who honor those who fear the Lord; who stand by their oath even to their hurt;	Simultaneous affirmation and confrontation; invitation to commitment; directive.
5 who do not lend money at interest, and do not take a bribe against the innocent. Those who do these things shall never be moved	Simultaneous affirmation and confrontation; invitation to commitment. Directive; implied directive.

The writer suggests a positive relationship in verse 1 by directly questioning God. We are immediately thrown into the action of the psalm and are encouraged to keep pace with the writer. The very nature of the question presupposes the idea that to abide in the tent of the Lord is a good thing to be desired. Because the question is asked initially, there is an element of implied drama. We question both our own ability and the writer's ability to abide with the Lord.

Verse 2 is written as if God had spoken an answer. By reading the text, we are vocalizing God's words while hearing them directed to us. Implicit is an indirect instruction for us to walk blamelessly and do what is right. This, we are told, is how to abide with the Lord. Since we have already agreed that we desire this action, there is an implicit directive contained here. Since God is answering our question, we can infer that we are cared about and have a direct relationship with God. We are also enticed to want closeness with God, and to strive to walk blamelessly.

A natural continuation of God's words being spoken is found in verse 3. This verse simultaneously affirms and confronts our behavior. We are affirmed if we are striving to refrain from slander and doing evil to our friends, and are not holding reproaches against our neighbors. At the same time, we are confronted when we are participating in these activities. Because of the way the author has indirectly stated that we need to refrain from these behaviors, we are encouraged in our abstinence. Even denial of our guilt invites more affirmation of these standards set by God. By virtue of our affirming these words, we are agreeing to the standard implied in the text. Either in the present or the future, the author has set the stage for our confrontation with sin to occur.

The writer has used the identical linguistic tools in verse 4 as in verse 3, yet different implied messages are communicated. "In whose eyes the wicked are despised" is another double-edged statement. It almost has the opposite effect, however, of verse 3. If we, as readers, hate our behaviors and condemn our actions, we are essentially siding with God, and by implication, being righteous. While on the surface, this idea appears to be condemning, it is also affirming at the implied level. The effect is powerful. In this verse, we are also encouraged to affirm our fear of the Lord and to desire to be influenced by God's directives.

Verse 5 also contains the same linguistic tools as verses 3 and 4. The implied message here directs us to refrain from lending at interest and taking bribes. The injunction referring to interest is found in Deut. 23:19-20. That passage prohibits us from lending at interest to a brother. The psalm writer did not mean to prohibit receiving any interest at all, so the average person reading this psalm is able to feel affirmed and not condemned for violating the standard. Although people who are taking bribes are aware of their guilt and feel chastised, most people reading this verse feel affirmed.

The final words have no verse number and, seem almost forced or peculiar when considered with the established order and pattern of the previous verses. The message is one of affirmation, commitment, and directive. All three ideas are conveyed in this one sentence. On the surface, the text communicates affirmation to those who follow the guidelines. There is an implication, however, for us to be affirming in our own commitment to abide by these guidelines. Also implicit is the directive that in adhering to the stated rules of behavior, we will be rewarded with strength and security.

Genesis

I ncoming inmates are segregated from the general population when they enter prison. They are living and learning about the institution and its rules with other "new inmates" while they become accustomed to their new environment. Inmates usually come into the prison with preconceived ideas about what will be expected of them in prison, and they are usually wrong. Their expectations usually are incorrect unless they have some previous experience of prison. This same type of projection is true for new staff members and for people visiting prison for the first time. The same also applies to preconceived ideas about hypnosis. When people are exposed to hypnosis for the first time, they are usually surprised to learn how different it is from what they had imagined. We cannot become prepared for the experience of hypnosis through popular culture or ideas in movies. Similar to prison, it most certainly becomes less scary once we are able to experience it.

If asked, most of the inmates would probably tell us that they believe God created the earth and the universe. It is likely that most Americans would answer in the same way. In fact, globally most people would agree. They may call their God by another name and believe in a different type of creation story, but most individuals agree to belief in God. It is interesting, however, that choosing to see that God had a hand in creation does not necessarily impact people's behavior. Even cold, antisocial, and criminally sophisticated people may state that they believe in God. If anything, believing in God can serve to insulate them from conscience or morality. Perhaps they say, "God and I have a special thing going." This statement is similar to a talisman that wards off attacks of conscience or refusing to recognize faults. It helps these persons in placing beliefs and actions in separate compartments. Persons who demonstrate faults the least usually hold the most rigid beliefs. I occasionally think that having a general belief without taking action is a hindrance to people. It seems to inoculate them from real beliefs that would bring about change and comfort. It has been my observation that inmates who claim to not believe in God have more of a sense of morality than ones who claim to believe but choose to remain inactive.

The opening passage in Genesis is so broad that most people can agree with it without much struggle of conscience. The passage embodies a general concept that is widely held, believed, and accepted. The passage also demonstrates the overall hypnotic concept of pace and lead. Pacing consists first of creating or discovering a common ground that allows identification or some connection.

As soon as we move beyond the first creation story, general agreement seems to wan. Were Adam and Eve the first people? This question is less broad and can quickly define people who believe in one way or the other. When Cain kills Able and takes a wife, the first real test of belief occurs. They are looking for reasons to agree or disagree. Some want to believe the Bible and find some way to understand the story of how Cain got his wife. If an individual decides not to believe, this story seems to mark the beginning. People tend to self-sort into two groups: believers who want to believe, and non-believers who choose not to believe. And people find reasons to strengthen their beliefs in either direction. It is really an individual decision. Each time a decision is made to go along with some new concept, a new decision is made to agree. For both the believer and the non-believer, the first perspective dictates what will be seen or not seen. These same phenomena occur in hypnosis. Once a connection is made through pacing, each turn that the hypnosis takes is one where the subject has to make a decision to continue the connection. However, if the general premise is accepted, then subsequent decisions are much easier. For instance, if we agree to go on a journey, deciding to pack our bags follows from our decision to go.

Many women begin to reach out to God in prison. Of course some are just the jailhouse religious variety that have little staying power. Others begin a journey that transforms their life. One woman who I will call Janet had grown up with abuse and neglect. She had been involved in a terrible crime where she took a person's life. Janet would have rather learned about nuclear physics than scripture. She had so much guilt about her crime that she stayed in trouble in prison. In fact, it was because of being in lockdown that she began to seek God. While alone, she slept as long as she could until she was forced to begin to face her life and the crime she had committed. As she did, she cried out to God to help her cope with the isolation and terrible loneliness of segregation, and to relieve her from the guilt she was carrying inside. Janet began to read the Bible, and she began to confess her sins to God. Through this process, she began to shed the shame of her past and became truly repentant of her actions. From that moment, Janet was sensitive to the Bible and faith as she sincerely changed her life. Because of the isolation, she received a fresh start. Janet moved toward God because she had no place else to go. She could no longer run from herself, her past, or her memories.

Another woman I will call Barbara was a wildcat who had committed terrible crimes. Although she did not kill, she had hurt, abused, and mentally tortured people to get drug money. Barbara seemed to care only about her next high, and she continued to act wild in prison. It was as if she knew that if she slowed down, she might have to face herself. One day her child who was visiting her asked, "Mommy, how come drugs are more important to you than I am?" Her child's words weighed heavy on her and she decided to make a 180-degree turn. As a result, Barbara became a pillar of the church and dramatically changed her appearance, actions, associations, and how she felt about herself. By the time she left prison, she had truly repented and transformed her life. Barbara has continued to do well.

I could tell story after story about women who have come to prison and transformed their lives. These types of stories would include inmates who had been hard and cruel, as well as those who had acted extremely passive and sensitive. Since both of these types of individuals made radical decisions and followed up their decisions with actions, they successfully maintained their changes. Yet no story can truly prepare us for seeing these types of changes occur. Personally observing someone who makes dramatic changes sends a message to us that we can also change. When we realize we need to make changes in our own lives, it becomes difficult to accept others who have chosen to make such transformations.

Lots of people, including prison inmates, begin reading the Bible with Genesis. Genesis appears to summon us, especially in the first few chapters. I think there are reasons why Genesis is inviting, in addition to the fact that it is the first book of the Bible. Genesis was not easy, however, to examine from the angle of hypnosis; in fact, it was the most difficult book of the Bible for me. The writer of Genesis uses a different style from other biblical writers who use hypnotic messages. The overall message of Genesis is broader, and the implied points can be difficult to identify with. Its power, however, can in one way be attributed to the fact that it is chronologically first. That Genesis covers all origins also aids in its powerfulness. Regardless of whether we literally or figuratively understand the verses, the writer's broader messages in the opening statements are difficult to avoid. Confusion techniques are not used, and there are no statements that suggest disassociation or amnesia. In fact, words are often stated in ways that invite remembrance. "Let there be light," and "in the beginning" are examples of compact phrases. "Let there be light" is memorable because it creates a milestone which directs where we will go in the future with the idea of a creator God beginning creation with words that we remember. Most students who study Hebrew are able to quote in Hebrew, "In the beginning God created...". Perhaps one of the reasons that students retain this bit of Hebrew while forgetting other passages is because of the strength contained in this particular text. This did not occur to me with my first reading of Genesis. I had to reread these verses numerous times in order to allow the hypnotic style to prod my thinking. The approaches, however, may be obvious to others at a first glance. It may also seem as if the characterizations are far reaching. At a minimum, I hope that I have understated the power of Genesis and its subtle form of hypnotic language.

A therapist friend of mine does not like the beginning phase of therapy with his new clients. For him, the initial work is always harder because he has to teach his client what he expects. He claims that he often teaches the client how he can be helpful while he simultaneously gathers data about the problem. My friend does have an important point. Beginnings are not easy. However, the initial seeds we sow are the ones we harvest later in the course of the therapy. In some ways, what we say in the beginning determines the course of the entire journey. First impressions are at times so lasting that they solidify what is expected and hoped for in the future. Other options are simply negated by virtue of the brightness of the initial light offered. Regardless of whether we are acting as ministers, therapists, or laypeople, our first impressions can be both positive and negative.

Prisoners often begin relationships that reflect all their past baggage. Their baggage influences who they select as friends, as well as how they approach others to become friends. Their fears restrict whom they see and whom they ignore. The inmates' biases tend to block them from viewing others realistically. They usually put their worst foot forward, even though they do not recognize that this is what they are doing. For instance, an alcoholic who is attempting to con others is most likely not winning friends and influencing people. This is especially true if he/she uses the same garden-variety con that every alcoholic has used before. These people are likely unaware that they are flaunting their worst side. If we really think about it, however, we are all like these prisoners. Usually, we try to put up our best display first. By hiding what and who we really are, we are actually only kidding ourselves. We are only attempting to direct how others see us. How refreshing it would be if, in the beginning, we could all simply accept that we are enough for others to really benefit from knowing us. Moving closer to others would certainly be easier. My therapist friend would also be much happier.

Genesis sets the stage for the rest of the book and yet built in is a faith test. I am reminded of Jesus' words in Luke 19:26: "I tell you, that to every one who has more will be given; but from him (her) who has not even what he (her) has will be taken away". If you approach Genesis with faith and want to find more, then you will. If you approach Genesis with no faith, then even that will likely be taken away. Essentially the key to be able to read Genesis is faith. If you adopt a faith perspective then one that is broadly looking for reasons to believe then you will find those reasons. While you might be drawn in by the language or something else, Genesis doesn't give up its secrets without the reader's willingness to begin with faith.

NRSV
Genesis 1:1-5

1:1 In the beginning when God created the heavens and the earth,	1:1: elicits expectancy, establishes rapport, implies a shared history and relationship, frames what follows.
2 the earth was a formless void and darkness covered the face of the deep, while a wind from God swept over the face of the waters.	1:2: paces, implies the symbol of problem, frames, continues to build rapport.
3 Then God said, "Let there be light"; and there was light.	1:3: frames intervention, establishes Rapport; problem solved; symbol frames book; mini drama.
4 And God saw that the light was good; and God separated the light from the darkness.	1:4: indirect suggestion; frames light and darkness; pacing; framing intervention; moves in minimal steps; elicits expectancy; symbolic double meaning; directive; seeding.
5 God called the light Day and the darkness he called Night. And there was evening and there was morning, the first day.	1:5: framing intervention; symbol of God's power; frame; disrupts flow.

Verse 1:1: "In the beginning" elicits expectancy. We are awaiting the next attraction. It is interesting to note that part of the expectancy that is established is done with the proposed questions that are left unanswered. For example, what and when is "the beginning"? Rapport is initially being built in this verse by an assumption that an established relationship exists. The writer speaks as if there is a shared history and relationship of caring and teaching. Implied is our importance since we are privy to this important information. Part of the inferred relationship is between us, the subject, and the storyteller. Since the writer begins in this way, the remainder of Genesis is framed within the context of us, as valuable readers, a creator God, and a caring narrator. The importance of the material is also implied, since the message is indirectly conveyed to us.

The pronouncement of events draws us into the created mental frame of this broad view. This broad view includes the idea that God created heaven, the world, and everything within the world. In effect, God created everything from nothing.

Verse 1:2: "The earth was a formless void and darkness covered the face of the deep, while a wind from God swept over the face of the waters." We want information, and the writer provides it. Pacing is established in an indirect manner, providing that we anticipate and want to be paced. After making contact in the first verse, we are now keeping pace with the author. This sentence can also be understood as one that describes a problem. While the formless earth with void represents the world, it also describes the emptiness we feel without God in our lives. Feeling formless without real definition and center is one of our central problems. Many people believe that the task in life is to face loneliness. It is also true that we need to face certain questions about our existence. Why are we here? What is our purpose? Perhaps we can also identify with the notion that darkness hides a barely perceivable spirit of the Lord moving near to our lives. Maybe we can also notice that it is in darkness or loneliness that God is near. If we agree, then we can recognize that the symbol of the problem is established. Our loneliness while searching for meaning in our lives is the essence of our problem.

Verse 1:3: "Then God said, 'Let there be light'; and there was light." The writer uses a framing intervention: God speaks light into existence. This technique emphasizes the powerfulness of God's words while suggesting that the Bible is God's word. In this way, rapport is being built. If we were honest about our own desires, most of us would say that we want our words to have a similar type of power. "Let there be light" is a commonly used phrase that people use when flipping light switches or using matches. The writer also embeds a command to us in this statement. The symbolism of spiritual light becomes more evident in the indirect message. By speaking about light, the writer solves the problem of darkness found in verse 2. The lack of form and the void in the darkness are solved by God when light is created. In this drama, we become alerted to the fact that the writer is speaking to us on multiple levels. In fact, the entire book of Genesis is framed in the light of the power of God's word while naming God as creator. There is also another theme occurring with the earth's formlessness and void. In this state that lacks God's presence and direction, the earth is connected to the darkness of evil and the formless void of materialism. It is God's presence and light that make the earth both habitable and livable. God's light will ultimately dispel the darkness.

Verse 1:4: "And God saw that the light was good; and God separated the light from the darkness." In this verse, the writer powerfully suggests that light is good. Light seems to be framed as right, or good, while darkness is viewed as bad. Certainly many of us today want to be sensitive to the racial implications that one may read into this type of statement where white is seen as the dominant culture. Since the superior culture for the original readers, and hearers was not white, it was obviously not a real consideration for these people. However, this early audience may have also read the sentence's context in the same way that we currently project our reality onto the words light and dark. There is the symbolism of darkness being connected to spiritual evil, and light to spiritual goodness. This symbolic device can serve as a pacing tool to agree with any reader's understanding. It can also serve as a mechanism to block pacing if the reader views light and dark as having racial meanings. This verse also contains an indirect message for us. Since God is going to separate the light from the darkness, we are being told, indirectly, to separate the light from the darkness in ourselves, too. We can infer that the writer is speaking about the natural separation that occurs between people with and without spiritual desires. It is common for us to separate ourselves from people who do not share our faith. The author further implies here that we are to be moving toward God and the light in others.

Verse 1:5: "God called the light Day, and the darkness he called Night. And there was evening, and there was morning, the first day." In this verse, the framing intervention is subtle. The day begins in the evening when God declares it to begin. Since God uses the labels night and day, the writer implies that we use terms God originally established. Another subtle shift in thought occurs with the pause that is established in verse 5. The four preceding verses flow from one thing to another. In verse five, a new pattern occurs: And then [pause] there was evening, and there was morning, the first day. The flow of this verse invites us to reflect, pause, and realize that a complete thought is being given. There is a pause after the first day of creation is completed. We can learn from this natural pause. What better time to reflect on what God has done during our day than when evening begins. Evening is also a good time to reflect on the upcoming day. Many people begin their next day with this type of preparation. Regardless of whether our preliminary decisions involve planning, packing lunches, or choosing clothing, preparation is a central part of the upcoming day's activities. Our day begins with how we anticipate it, and our plans or lack of plans. Attitude is crucial to how we interpret events. There is a big difference between when we anticipate finding new learning or understanding about our relationship to God, and those times when we expect to have the same old day as the one just expired. Regardless of how we think of our day beginning, it can become mundane with sameness. Taking responsibility for preparing how we will begin our day is a wonderful way to factor in joy, newness, and creativity.

Revelation

Knowing about end-time prophecies is certainly a hot topic in prison settings. A believable and entertaining Bible study on the book of Revelation would most likely be popular. Perhaps people in prison want to make sure that they are right with God before the end of time. They may be worried about their sins and may desire the comfort of knowing about their future. It is also probable that prisoners seek knowledge-as-power, but they may also be like the average individual who seeks definitive answers to the complex question concerning the end of time.

I was frequently asked questions pertaining to Revelation and the end-time when I began working in the women's prison. It seemed that everyone wanted to know how to understand this particular text. Even as I armed myself with commentaries about the book of Revelation, I discovered that there was not much agreement among the authors of these commentaries. Each of the commentaries emphasized different aspects, and many of these books were difficult to interpret. Even more of a challenge for me was to communicate an author's ideas to individuals with little or no theological background.

Perhaps people in prison are more aware of their sins and the awfulness of punishment. For individuals who have taken someone else's life, a special knowledge of eternal punishment exists. They know the depth and length to which sins can be carried, as well as the regret that one can feel when wishing actions could be reversed. Drug addicts carried an awareness of their death. Many had overdosed at least once, or had lost a friend. In either case, addicts seemed to carry more of an awareness of facing themselves and eternal punishment than the average person. Maybe they were more cognizant of judging themselves.

Many of the women who were more insightful and aware were also more popular.

Credit may also be given to the prison and the court system for helping individuals to be more aware of judgment. It has been my observation that many of the inmates were reared in either rigid and conservative religious homes, or in non-religious settings where morals and accountability had been lax. Prisoners who had been reared in average religious settings, rather than these extreme cases, were rare. It is understandable that at both ends of the spectrum, people were sensitized about Revelation and the end-time.

Many prisoners also revealed fears of dying in prison. Few seemed to carry their fears outside of prison walls. Some felt that death in prison would be too lonely. Others wanted to avoid the stigma that they believed would be cast on their families and themselves. Still others emphatically stated that they were not afraid to die except in prison. Perhaps their fears were connected to shame, final judgment, or facing how they have lived. I have entertained the idea that these fears were irrational and were based on how we believe death should be rather than how it actually occurs in America. To die in prison involves having others around us who know and are concerned about us. Dying in a nursing home at the end of a long life may be a more lonely experience than if one died in prison. In fact, I suspect that the average hospital death is lonelier. Yet, fear is personal and does not need to be rational. The fear of dying in prison has motivated a number of women to live longer than I believe they would have if they had not hoped to die as free women. If being aware of the book of Revelation and of the end-time motivates us to live more appropriately today, I see that as a blessing. It is an awareness that is open to all of us, both in and outside prison walls.

The first three women I met at the prison who died there are vivid in my memory. The first inmate had a long history of drug addiction. She came to prison willing to change and worked hard on overcoming her addictions and making herself appropriate for society. This woman was a strong leader in a therapy group I led at the prison. Since she was older, she became a mother figure to a number of other women. One day after she arrived in her unit after group, she dropped dead from a massive heart attack. All of us who knew and cared about her were deeply bothered by her death. I found myself searching my own actions to see if I could have done anything differently while she was alive. It was a time when all of us who knew her became aware of our own mortality. It was as if she had secretly known that her time was short and that she needed to use it wisely. Her last days on earth used her faith, insight, and role as an older woman who helped others. It was a joy to watch her turn her life around and become this kind of inspiration.

The other two inmates who died were less fortunate because they did not make positive changes. Their lives ended abruptly from hidden medical problems. Even though all three women brought on their early deaths by their lifestyles, each of their deaths resulted in a different learning. The second woman was young and died suddenly in her sleep. Her last days were filled with business as usual, and she had refrained from making changes. While her death was tragic, it did not motivate us to examine our own lives or the reality of death. It was as if her life of denial was also evident in her death. The third inmate followed a similar pattern to the second. At the prison, she refused to change personally and became involved mostly in her own pleasures. While secluding herself from family and friends, she had little impact on others. Her death brought only the momentary self-reflection that someone related to the prison had died. Inmates afraid of dying in prison were impacted only because of their own fears. Her lifestyle eclipsed her from having a positive effect on others' lives. People ignored her death in the same way that she had ignored them in life.

While I believe that I have learned a tremendous amount from all of the inmates, and especially from those who have died, I still do not comprehend the book of Revelation. End-time predictions that seem to run from one extreme to the other are difficult to understand. The only ones that make sense to me are the ones that involve the deaths of people I have known. These experiences have impacted me since they invite me to examine myself. Since the experts do not seem to agree about the form, style, or content of what is to be learned from the prophecies, my efforts to comprehend the book of Revelation seem to have been fruitless.

The book of Revelation has so much more to offer us than just end-time predictions. In fact, in the wake of the millennium, these prophecies have taken on a different character. Specifically, there is no longer the type of fear driving people's desire to know what would happen before the crucial year 2000.

The verses in Revelation 22:17-21 assume that you have faith and that you are willing to operate on that faith. Furthermore, there is a wide scope of meaning that is implied. It would be difficult on the basis of the language structure of the book of Revelation to argue for or against any of the popular methods of interpreting Revelation. In fact, the language almost assumes that the way you are interpreting the passage is the correct one, and that you are only instructed not to add to it or take away from it. Yet one invitation seems to be present in the text about how to read the book, that is with your faith it will be correct if you assume it is for you, and not for general consumption. We are told to not add to or take away from this text. It is almost assumed that you will receive through your faith messages that are relevant to you.

Lots of folks balk at reading the book of Revelation because they think they are supposed to understand the hidden meaning about the end of the world. Since that isn't easily accomplished, many people find the book of little value and almost a sign of their not having strong faith. That isn't fair. Recognize that the meanings can be more personal and can be understood with a willingness to allow the text to speak to you about you. Zen Buddhism has a concept about life learnings that could assist the reader at this point. It is a concept that is invited by the symbolism and abstractness of Revelation 22:17-21. The concept can be understood this way: A young female soccer player had discovered she had weak ankles. In order to improve her ankle strength and to make her a better soccer player the coach prescribed an exercise. The prescription was to balance on a cylinder on one leg while returning serves with the other leg. She recognized that there were life lessons in the practice. She understood that balance strengthens. She also understood that developing more balance in her life made her both a better soccer player as well as human being. It would strengthen her mentally, emotionally, and spiritually.

NRSV
Revelation 22:17-21

17 The Spirit and the bride say, "Come." And let everyone who hears say, "Come." And let everyone who is thirsty come. Let anyone who wishes take the water of life as a gift.	22:17: Interspersal; rapport; directive; indirect suggestion; subtle congratulation; future orientation; rapport; ratifies change; frame; directive symbol and post-hypnotic symbol.
18 I warn everyone who hears the words of the prophecy of this book: if anyone adds to them, God will add to that person the plagues described in this book;	22:18: Indirect message; indirect suggestion; elicits motivation; directive given; task given that consolidates learning.
19 if anyone takes away from the words of the book of this prophecy, God will take away that person's share in the tree of life and in the holy city, which are described in this book.	22:19: indirect message; indirect suggestion; future orientation; elicits motivation; directive given; task given that consolidates learning.
20 The one who testifies to these things says, "Surely I am coming soon." Amen. Come, Lord Jesus!	22:20: Future orientation; ratify changes; indirect message; ratify changes a second time.
21 The grace of the Lord Jesus be with all the saints. Amen.	22:21 ratifies changes; congratulates reader on position; elicits motivation.

Verse 17: "The Spirit and the bride say, 'Come.'" While the spirit and the bride's word, come, encourages Jesus to return, the declaration invites us, as readers, to show up as well. There is a good example of the interspersal technique contained in the next sentence when the author bids all who hear to say, "Come." The idea of coming implies commitment or resolution as a secondary meaning. The writer simply

states the surface meaning. We are invited to commit more deeply with the implied meaning.

Rapport is being built within an increasingly wider scope and meaning of the formula that progresses from the Spirit and the bride to everyone who hears, and finally to all who are thirsty. We must be able to hear in order to get the writer's message. Listening is implied as a positive characteristic. If we do not hear or understand, then the message is not for us. Yet, who has not been thirsty at one time or another? It follows that regardless of whether we are people who can hear, we need to sense the deeper meaning found in this passage. A universality of this verse is its comparison to a fishing net that encompasses all who are near. While the surface meaning is abstract, hear has a double meaning when used in this sentence. Whoever thirsts for the truth and for Jesus' return is instructed to come. At another level, anyone who is or has been thirsty can accept the writer's invitation to come. Rapport is being built here with the inclusion. At the same time, we are directed to come at least twice, and maybe even three times. The first time the directive comes from the Spirit and the bride when they state, "Come." This same directive is issued three times. We are given an indirect suggestion to desire Jesus' return, as well as, an indirect message to invite others to come. We are also instructed to wish taking the water of life as a gift. The author implies for us to wish it while at the same time, he directs us to take it. A subtle congratulation occurs with the writer's inclusion of us. This is an indirect congratulation since the inclusion is implied.

Since verse 17 is focused on where the coming will occur in the future, we are also subtlety invited to think about a particular focus in the future. This involves centering our attention and thinking about where Jesus is coming.

Changes that we have made or are committed to making are ratified in subtle ways in these last verses. In verse 17, the message of ratifying previous events is partly created by context. By placing verse 17 at the end of the book of Revelation, the writer gives the directive to come while congratulating us on already making our decision to be included. As mentioned, this technique subtly confirms our decision to come. Another subtle ratification occurs with the author attempts to move us from being invited to come to being invited to say, "Come" ourselves. We are now extended an invitation to be a part of the invitational committee. In other words, if we are invited to participate in a function, and then we accept a second proposal to be a part of the inviting committee, we have solidified our commitment from one of an attendee to that of an active participant or recruiter.

A framing intervention is another technique that is effectively used in verse 17. Simply defined, this is an intervention that casts an idea, thing, event, or person in a particular light. It is more than what politicians refer to as spin, because it used to help and assist rather than manipulate. While this type of device may cast an idea in a particular light that the writer endorses, it is also used to aid us. In this particular verse, the author uses several frames. The command come is emphasized when the Spirit and the bride say, "Come." The mention of the name of the Spirit and the bride also underscores the word and the importance of whom the author is referring to. The weight and credibility of the Spirit and bride are evoked to magnify the word in the same way that repeating the command come places an emphasis on the word. A subtler framing example is found in the phrase "let everyone who desires take the water of life as a gift." That the water of life is free to all who desire it emphasizes a future involving the afterlife. This statement also suggests to us that listening to the writer is important if we desire to participate in the afterlife. For those of us who read the book and desire this gift, we are given a present. The writer implies that we have the right to be an insider and that we are accepted if we desire it. This idea of acceptance to be claimed replaces any emphasis on legalism.

The water of life is symbolic of many different things occurring at the same time. It can be interpreted simultaneously as meaning life, thirst quenching, satisfying, pure,and cleansing. Since the writer uses water at the end of the book of Revelation, its context allows for the word to be a post-hypnotic symbol. For instance, water that is seen and used either while or after dwelling upon the reading emphasizes the word after we leave this text to engage in another activity.

Verse18: "I warn everyone who hears the words of the prophecy of this book: if any one adds to them, God will add to that person the plagues described in this book." Because the warning is so strict in this verse, the writer implies that the words themselves are extremely important. Making additions to the words is compared to the trickery used by the serpent in Genesis when he added to the words that God had said to Eve.

Another indirect suggestion found in this passage comes from carefully using accurate and repeated tellings and understandings of this book. A way to verify others' comments about prophecy is also contained here. Thus, commentators who add to the words in order to fit their schemes are ones whose interpretations need to be questioned. It is obvious that the directive given in this verse is for us to refrain from adding to the prophecy of the book of Revelation. This edict encourages us to remember the plagues of verse 18.

Verse 19: "if anyone takes away from the words of the book of this prophecy, God will take away that person's share in the tree of life and in the holy city, which are described in this book." Again, the writer indirectly reiterates the importance of the words. This message is intensified with its repetition from verse 18. Since the focus of the warning, like Jesus' coming, is placed in the future, we are oriented to the future.

The author elicits motivation from what we can either avoid or attain by revising the words of the prophecy. A more general motivation, however, is to desire the water of life and to attain the holy city. We are once again directed to leave the book of prophecy as it is. With the writer's warning of a different punishment in the future, we are also invited to recall the promises of the future if we are faithful. Indirectly, the writer proposes that we reaffirm our commitment to God and God's word.

Verse 20: "The one who testifies to these things says, 'Surely I am coming soon.' Amen. Come, Lord Jesus!" The first part of this sentence contains a double meaning, perhaps even a triple meaning. On the surface, the writer speaks about the one who testifies to these things. There is a greater emphasis placed on the words by the person who states them on this level. From a deeper prospective, it is difficult to read this passage and refrain from testifying, since we are saying and affirming the words in our minds while we read them. Since our role as readers is emphasized, a case can also be made that this is a subtle form of the writer's ratification of changes. The second part of the sentence, "surely…" invites us to focus in the future. When this type of orientation occurs directly after an emphasis on a commitment, or an acceptance of a concept found in the beginning of a sentence, the initial suggestion is going to be buried in our unconscious minds. In other words, it is most probable that we will accept the deeper, initial proposal without disagreement. "Surely…" indirectly suggests that we be ready. We have inside information and we are treated as someone who is on the side of the one who testifies.

"Amen. Come Lord Jesus!" encourages us to ratify our position and participate. The writer assures us that we can both count on and look forward to the time when Jesus will surely come. "Come Lord Jesus" ratifies our position since we are now doing what the author suggested that we do in verse 17. In saying the words in our minds, and reading them, we are both affirming and believing in the statement. Our position that we previously adopted is being confirmed.

21 "The grace of the Lord Jesus be with all the saints. Amen." We are both receiving and pronouncing a blessing on all the saints, with the writer. We are invited to do this even if we do not feel worthy. Desiring it for others ratifies our own belief that to be considered, accepted, and pronounced a saint is a good thing, regardless of how we feel. If we are able to receive the blessing because of grace; however, then our transformed value system is confirmed. In either event, we are indirectly congratulated on our position. This occurs when we either

ratify the writer's words or receive the blessing. Motivation is elicited in both of these instances. We become encouraged either in our Christian walk, or in our ability to allow ourselves the opportunity to receive the blessing.

Ruth

T he story of Ruth is memorable because of Ruth's faith, determination, and good fortune. While the book of Ruth itself is short, it carries deep wisdom. For this reason alone, Ruth truly deserves an important place in Judeo-Christian thought. The more that we, as readers, study this book, the more we will gain while recognizing its potential. A different dimension can be added to our understanding when we learn that Ruth, as a Moabite, was from a culture of people who were hated and despised by the Jews for their practice of child sacrifice. This information becomes even more intriguing when we consider that Ruth was in the lineage of Jesus.

Many women who come to prison have faced terrible tragedies of the kind that Ruth and Naomi had faced. Because of their traumas, many come to see prison as a sanctuary. One particular woman stands out in my mind. During an 18-month period before she committed her crime, this individual experienced an overwhelming number of tragedies. She lost her parents and only sister in a gruesome accident, her husband divorced her for another woman, and one of her three children killed his older sibling with a gun that this woman had purchased for protection. It was during this point in time when a narcotics agent asked her if she could help him get some drugs. She mindlessly took his money and purchased the drugs for him. Even though she had no prior history of drug use or drug sales, this woman was convicted and sentenced to prison. I have never been able to understand whether the judge who sentenced her was kind, cruel, or naive. Coming to prison was one of the best things that could have happened to this woman. In addition to finding a sanctuary from all of her losses, she also received training and counseling. While courageously accepting all of her tragedies was difficult for this woman, her tragedies resulted in her restored belief in God.

A number of women come to prison because of their loyalty to a mother or father who also went to prison, and who either died or deserted them. It is almost as if these inmates cannot stop their own self-destructive behavior until they can redeem the memory of their parent by coming to prison. One woman I will call Reba came to prison because of drug use. Although her father had been in prison when she was a little girl, she still looked up to him because they favored one another and because Reba remembered him as being kind to her. Reba's mother had never forgiven her father for going to prison and leaving her and Reba to support themselves. After remarrying, Reba's mother inadvertently did not see how her continual comparisons of Reba to her father had a negative effect. In addition to the comparisons, Reba's physical characteristics led Reba to believe that she and her father looked very much alike. Things that she heard about her father seemed to be her destiny. Unfortunately, Reba's case is a common.

The book of Ruth contains only four chapters. It demonstrates, however, the ways in which all of the books of the Bible use hypnotic devices to recount events. Ruth is filled with hypnotic tools that positively impact us. We are encouraged to have more faith, respect women, and believe that God rewards those who love the Lord and follow the law. The story uses drama while moving in minimal steps. Ruth contains numerous implied meanings, messages of faith, and indirect directives. Overall, the writer of Ruth implies that God will bless us through the community of believers and that a restorative justice will happen for those of us who have faith. Even individuals who find themselves merely associated with believers will be blessed.

The familiar words, "Where you go, I will go; where you lodge, I will lodge; your people shall be my people, and you're God my God," are very powerful and hypnotic words. When we read these words that Ruth said to Naomi, we are also saying the words and making a commitment to ourselves. Perhaps this is the reason this verse has been used so often to convey a sense of commitment both in ceremonies and in dramatic moments where people need reassurance. The entire book elicits expectancy through implying that this type of blessing can happen to any of us. Ruth did not hold a special right to these blessings. In fact, Ruth, from her genetic birth, was not entitled to receive any of them. She did evoke a right, however, by her faithfulness in obeying the spirit of the law by looking after Naomi. Ruth also continued her faith and her willingness to become one with the community of believers.

With its compact number of hypnotic tools, Ruth is not typical of every book of the Bible. It does represent, however, the ways in which the stories recounted in the Bible use hypnotic devices. Events recounted in Genesis, Numbers, Samuel, Judges, and Exodus, to name a few, all contain hypnotic devices. Linguistically, we can diagram, direct, and detail how these books instill, evoke, and rebuke us. None of our analysis, however, can detract from the amazing power of the Bible. Our analysis confirms the sacredness of the scriptures even more. This is because other books do not contain a significant number of devices that serve to uplift, empower, and teach, and instill faith and positive standards.

Instead of displaying the entire book of Ruth and noting those places where hypnotic devices appear, the devices are listed along with observations about how they appear in the text. Hopefully, this order makes the task more easily understood and manageable. These concepts are adapted from the list of hypnotic techniques mentioned in the Introduction and offered by Dr. Jeffrey Zeig, director of the Milton H. Erickson Foundation. The list is entitled GIFT-WRAPPING AND PROCESSING.

The language structure seems to invite reading as you would a novel, a story, or the newspaper. In short, the messages are delivered in-between the lines subtly. The effect is likely to be of a positive effect. This would be a good book for people to read who are long beyond any earlier struggle and who have come through reasonably safe. It would be an encouragement for those types of folks, who had been through crises or a trauma. It wouldn't assist the person struggling with their faith who was also in the midst of a crisis. The happy ending is almost too unbelievable for a person in the throes of crisis and experiencing a faith struggle.

These are the hypnotic techniques that the writer of Ruth uses, with a discussion of each:

Pacing: Pacing involves the concept of respect and means that we are to begin where clients are by being in step with them. If we, for example, want to influence others, we must first be willing to pace with or be on a similar level with them. Pacing communicates respect because another person's position is acknowledged as important. In addition, other persons are recognized as having value. Telling a story that enables us to identify with another person is one of the ways that pacing is effectively used. The story of Ruth captures our attention, and we are able to identify with Ruth at several levels. Perhaps we can identify with Naomi and her husband's need to go to a foreign country during a time of famine. Ruth, Boaz, Naomi, and the townspeople are also characters that we may resonate with at some level. We may also simultaneously identify with Ruth as she overcomes obstacles and with Naomi as she receives unanticipated blessings from others.

Establishing Rapport: Establishing Rapport also communicates reverence to us when a writer respects our way of hearing, learning, being, and seeing. In other words, the most effective way that a writer communicates with us is by speaking in a language that we understand. It is the writer's way of saying that we have commonality. We generally feel rapport with another person when we sense that we are understood in our commonality. In reference to the book of Ruth, we can identify with one or more of the characters can and feel understood by the writer of Ruth. The writer has established rapport.

Tricks used to generate artificial rapport simply do not work and are usually insulting. For example, the average preacher who uses his/her past sin to force artificial rapport with prisoners is degrading the audience rather than relating to the audience. An inmate who has killed a child carries different feelings of guilt than does someone who has been issued a traffic violation. For the preacher to tell the inmate that he/she understands is insulting. Our experiences obviously cannot be the same. Informing others that we can understand their plight sounds disrespectful. On the other hand, allowing others to decide if we can understand is affirming.

Congratulation: To congratulate a person on his/her position is a technique employed for the tasks of rapport building, reframing, and pacing. Honesty, however, is required with this particular mechanism. Even those of us who are not regarded as highly intelligent can easily see through dishonest compliments. We may not confront the dishonesty, but we know at some level when someone is attempting to manipulate us. Honest appreciation for our position, however, does help us to feel understood and appreciated. In Ruth, we are indirectly congratulated for being readers, and we are invited to feel understood and valued for our difficulties and struggles. This is a subtle and pervasive concept found in this story.

Elicit motivation: In order to do this effectively, we must first respect others enough to understand what motivates them, as well as what blocks their motivation. It is important to note that we need to refrain from judgment in this type of relating. Understanding, compassion, and wisdom are necessary attributes. The author of Ruth elicits motivation for those of us who are believers and who follow the law. Our motivation is also increased if we desire to become a member of or to strengthen our ties with a community of believers. This occurs indirectly as we identify with Ruth's and Naomi's struggles and successes. In this way, we have hope, with our faith, of overcoming our situation like Ruth and Naomi did.

Elicit expectancy: Generating a hopeful outcome for the future is powerful. Stated yet another way, "Expectancy is the mother of tomorrow." Our expectations have a strong way of coming to pass. If we believe that it is possible to overcome our problems and if we believe that successful solutions are on their way, then we are expecting positive outcomes. Generating a positive expectation often depends upon the attitude of the speaker and his/her success stories. If someone we know and like believes in our ability to overcome obstacles, it is likely that we will feel a positive expectancy.

Since all of the believers in Ruth receive blessings, an implied message is that blessings occur for believers. That our steadfastness will be rewarded with unforeseen blessings is another message, since the blessings in Ruth occur after tragedy and times of struggle. The writer indirectly says that these unknown blessings will often come through the community of believers and through our obedience to the laws set down by God.

Seed intended targets: This technique recognizes the idea that one thought often prompts other thoughts regarding the same subject. For example, raising the idea of a delicious meal that is lovingly prepared can evoke thoughts about hunger, former meals, or guilt. One who states that he/she is hungry can also raise thoughts about our level of hunger. Commercials frequently use this technique by leading us to think about items we were not aware that we wanted, so that they can sell us what we didn't know existed. In therapy, the device is often used to assist persons in becoming able to think again about what has frightened them. Stories about a particular path to success seed either the idea of accomplishment or types of strategies that lead to success.

Since Ruth is read within the context of the overall Bible, hope and positive expectancy are generated for us. God is seen as faithful and rewarding. Outside of the Bible's context, Ruth can be viewed as having a personal responsibility in a hostile world. The writer also implies that there are several ways to achieve positive outcomes. For example, we are often blessed when we do for others. Since the book of Ruth is particularly positive, there are a number of concepts that are considered to be seeding for future growth and development.

Framing intervention: Reframing is a concept that recognizes the idea that our thinking changes when we consider a different context or frame of reference. Reframing for a person whose attitude is self-defeating is simply giving back to the person the ability to think effectively. For instance, when we feel defeated, everything in our world seems overwhelming. On the other hand, when we find ourselves fresh from a success, we see the same challenge as another opportunity to shine, succeed, or have a good time. The frame in which we view our world either distorts or clarifies what we see. Some frames of reference preclude other ones. When we are depressed and feeling failure, we are not likely to view challenges as opportunities.

The entire book of Ruth frames, or reframes, tragedy. It is viewed as a time when our faith can help us to be blessed. Perhaps we have been unable to see these ways before. The writer also frames faithfulness and loyalty as more than virtues. They are seen as a road to peace and happiness, and to respectable inclusion in the community of faith.

Moving in minimal strategic steps: This approach acknowledges that a respectful way of working with others is by recognizing that others' pace may be influenced by fears and unknown memories. This concept also acknowledges that minimal changes in others' ability to complete a task greatly assists in the achievement of goals. It may or may not be an exaggeration to state that Ruth moves in minimal steps from her tragedy to her choice of loyalty and devotion to Naomi. Ruth continues gradually as she follows Naomi's directions and later attracts Boaz as her protector and husband.

Create drama: This device heightens the final effect of the story and what the story's writer ultimately wants to communicate. Drama increases interest while inviting us into the proposed frame of reference with its resolution. It respects our need to be entertained. Information and ideas are effectively communicated in ways that respect our interest level. As Mary Poppins said, "A spoonful of sugar makes the medicine go down." In similar ways, the use of dramas, stories, and metaphors are respectful to us by placing the information in a form we can easily swallow. The story of Ruth clearly uses drama to communicate important ideas and beliefs about our faith, the community of faith, and the ways in which God works to redeem and transform.

Establish a symbol of the problem: This technique uses the manner in which symbolic experiences impact our lives in significant ways. For example, the more we identify with a sports team, the more the team's victory or defeat can affect our moods. We invest much of our energy and self-esteem in symbols that ultimately hurt us. In order to help us, it is appropriate that therapists recognize ways that symbols can also instill within us hope and the recognition of our successful abilities. Ruth and Naomi's struggles and losses can become a symbol of our struggles and losses. The more that we identify with their struggles, the more we also identify with their successes.

Empathy story: This concept respects the fact that we identify with others through our shared commonalties. When we read scripture, we give and take equally from the text. Our attitudes, frames of reference, moods, and beliefs affect what we are able to see. As we change, we view the same scripture differently, because we bring a new perspective to the text. We are similarly impacted by our identification with the characters. A story that helps us to feel understood and less lonely, also contributes to our feelings of hope and connectedness. Ruth and Naomi's story is one that both allows and advocates empathy. We are encouraged to identify with Ruth, Naomi, Boaz, the deceased husbands, and the community people. Since Ruth, Naomi, and Boaz are obvious, elaboration here would be redundant. The deceased husbands and the townspeople; however are treated with respect, even though they are marginal characters. This particular identification serves as an encouragement for the forgotten and shy reader to also feel important.

Indirect suggestion: Indirect suggestion is a technique that emphasizes maintaining and enhancing a person's self-esteem. Indirect suggestion gives the receiver the choice of accepting or rejecting the idea without becoming involved in a power struggle with the sender. Indirect suggestion also respects the receiver's pride by allowing him/her to be involved in making decisions. These suggestions are given to us throughout the Bible. The emphasis may be seen in what happens to people who sin without remorse, and to the righteous ones who show repentance for their sins. Ruth contains many indirect ideas. The more obvious ones refer to trusting God and receiving blessings. Both Ruth's and Naomi's examples of trusting in God and going to the community of faith to receive support tell us indirectly that we can receive support from a faith community. We can trust God to reward those of us who diligently seek God. Naomi, with her faith, is rewarded in her relationship with Ruth, the community, her extended family, and God. Ruth's actions show us how to be faithful in our deeds.

Reframing: Reframing, or giving something a positive connotation, is a technique that recognizes how an idea is framed. In other words, the way an idea is received impacts how it will be understood. The following example demonstrates this point. An inmate who was adopted as a child grew up realizing that her parents' decision to give her away was based on financial difficulties. This woman consequently carried much shame about the fact that she was her parents' only child who was put up for adoption. She shared this experience and her feelings of shame with her therapy group. The woman was reminded that she and Moses were both chosen from among many to be adopted. With time, the woman stopped feeling shame and developed pride about who she was. The woman reframed her understanding of her family and childhood. Her new interpretation allowed her to view her adoption as an event that made her special. Her shyness, which resulted from shame, also diminished. She became more active and outgoing. Before her parole, she led her group and helped other women to let go of childhood shame.

The book of Ruth reframes the average reader's ideas. For example, a female convert is the hero of the story rather than a Jewish male. Ruth offers a positive frame of reference for people who carry negative thoughts about converts, Moabites, or women. In addition, readers who see tragedy as a sign of God's displeasure are given a more neutral way of understanding tragedy. Exactly what Ruth reframes for us depends on what we bring to the story. The themes of overcoming hardship, alienation, and social status can occur through the community of believers by adhering to faith, laws, and traditions.

Ordeals: Ordeals are events that are used by a therapist in order to help clients achieve their goals. Clients are encouraged to move through, or find themselves in, a particular situation. Typically, it is an event that prompts internal change for the client by rearranging the client's thoughts about self. For example, when we think of near-death experiences, usually we view them in terms of rearranging our priorities and altering our values. Encountering major crises causes us to rethink our lives. Ordeals are usually not explained by the therapist to a client. Clients need to supply their own meanings to strange events, in order to make sense of their world. The story of Ruth is comprised of Ruth and Naomi's ordeals. These women endured losses, hardships, prejudices, poverty, and more. In effect, their worlds were turned upside-down. In the process of restructuring their lives, however, Ruth and Naomi discovered meaning, community, and safety. As we move with them, either through empathy or identification, we can notice how our thoughts are also reordered and re-evaluated.

Future orientation: Future orientation refers to the act of thinking about the future in order to alter a current experience. In this way, present difficulties may be overcome. The process remains the same, regardless of whether it happens spontaneously or with the direction of a therapist. The following example illustrates this technique. Inmates, who regularly think about their release, do this in order to cope with their present feelings of guilt or loneliness. When we bring our own hopelessness from current tragedies, we can also regain hope from the inspiring ending of the story of Ruth. Future orientation is occurring when we begin to think about how God can and will help us in the future.

Fantasy Rehearsal: This is a type of fantasy that results from rehearsing a successful outcome from a problem. Occasionally, this technique occurs spontaneously. At other times, a book, movie, story, or therapist encourages fantasy rehearsal. When this device is used in a hypnotic fashion, it is a way of implying that we already have certain abilities that we imagine ourselves as having in the future. In fact, part of the intention in using our imagination for future options is to supplant the self-doubt that keeps us from doing what we can already do. It is merely using a positive fantasy to counteract a negative fantasy of fear. The story of Ruth allows us to use the uplifting ending as a way of thinking more positively about our faith, our community, or the possibilities of what can happen through or beyond tragedy. It is important to note that this device is not intended to stimulate action or thought immediately. Rather, it is a method of planting seeds for future thoughts.

Metaphors: Metaphors are stories or ideas that indirectly offer solutions. A metaphor respects our sense of pride and independence. When a metaphor is used, we can choose to use the solution and not feel indebted to those giving the advice. In addition, we can feel proud of finding the answer ourselves, even though a similar solution is hinted at or offered with the metaphor. Ruth offers several metaphors about successfully coping with adversity and overcoming hardship. It also offers a way for us to be rewarded for our faith.

Symbols: Symbols stand in for people, places, things, or ideas. As such, they are ambassadors for new concepts or new ways of behaving. Symbols are used all the time to communicate our perceptions. Words are symbols. Anything used for representation can become a symbol. When a symbol of shame becomes healed, fixed, or overcome, our self-esteem increases. Athletic teams, for instance, become our symbols; when "our team" wins or loses, we can also feel the victory or defeat.

Another common example with symbols can be observed in parents who allow their children to represent themselves. Parents often do this outside of their own awareness, regardless of whether they are living vicariously through their children. If someone does not like the parent's child, then that parent tends to believe that this same person does not like him or her. On the other hand, when someone treats the parent's child well, they feel good towards that person. The tragedies Ruth and Naomi experienced as a result of the death of people they loved can be symbolic of the losses in our own lives. Perhaps we feel bad because of a death or because of our poverty following a death. Since Ruth's shame was transformed, her story can also speak to our shame.

Anecdotes: Anecdotes are stories that teach a principle or a particular lesson. When we read the Bible, it is clear that the biblical writers used stories to convey truths and to teach principles of living. Therapists use anecdotes for the same reason. Since the messages are indirect and can more easily bypass resistance, hypnosis uses them frequently. Anecdotes help the hearer to use information rather than become stuck at being told what to do. A difference between anecdotes and metaphors is that the metaphors attempt to symbolize some aspect of the person hearing the story. Anecdotes attempt to teach a point and may not necessarily be representing anything about the individual hearing the story.

Interspersal technique: Milton H. Erickson was famous for developing interspersal technique as a form of indirect and covert communication. This mechanism uses the fact that two separate messages can be communicated in one sentence. It also is based on the truth that voice tone, emphasis, and implied meanings underscore communication. Without an example, this concept may seem both difficult to grasp and complex to describe. However, we may already know more about this technique than we think, especially as we listen to ourselves. This is because we continuously use these tools. Double messages are often implicit in what is said to us. When we listen to inferred messages, we can notice them if we allow ourselves enough time to hear them.

There are no good examples of this interspersal technique in Ruth. However, there is an occurrence found in Ruth 2:4, provided that we are willing to see it as interspersal technique. Verse 2:4 reads, "and behold, Boaz came from Bethlehem. He said to the reapers, 'The Lord be with you!' And they answered, 'The Lord bless you.'" This interspersal technique incorporates a hypnotic command in an innocent fashion, similar to quoting someone who says, "Get the idea! It is one we can use." In reference to verse 2:4, we are able to receive blessings from both Boaz and the reapers. Numerous other passages in the Bible also demonstrate examples of the interspersal technique. If we are looking closely at a writer's words, we can notice how often this mechanism is used. It is a way that we can be told how important that we are at an unconscious level. In this manner, it is unnecessary for our conscious mind to believe the positive compliments the author gives us about ourselves.

It is hoped that it is clear that the story of Ruth uses many linguistic techniques that are used in hypnosis. These mechanisms are effective tools for communicating and represent useful parts of language. Stories of the Bible contain many examples of these powerful language devices.

What Does All of This Mean?

W hat does all of this mean? It means that if it is true that the Bible is filled with hypnotic techniques, then looking for the "one message" of a passage misses the point. When we allow the scriptures to impact us, we will receive the message of the text. In effect, we can allow our left-brain to experience the words while our right-brain grasps the reality in an artistic fashion based on our emotional needs at any given point. Biblical text is and always will be alive. Part of our being alive signifies that no one can own, possess, or even truly claim that they have the one and only way of interpreting any particular passage.

It took me a long time to be able to understand how criminally minded people could read and dismiss scripture before committing crimes. I now realize that individuals who live in denial and are disassociating can truly pigeonhole information. When we let ourselves experience the trance of scripture, however, we are able to use and to receive the messages of the Bible in different ways. Scripture can come alive each and every time we encounter it.

Evangelicals are quick to quote Hebrew 4:12-13: "For the word of God is living and active, sharper than any two-edge sword, piercing to the division of soul and spirit, of joints and morrow and discerning the thoughts and intentions of the heart. And before him no creature is hidden, but all are open and laid bare to the eyes of him with whom we have to do." Reading the scriptures with only the left-brain, logical side does not allow the mystical aspects of the right-brain to experience the interactional slant of scripture.

The text comes alive because the hypnotic aspects interact with our faith and with us—in other words, what we bring to the passage.

When we bring our faith and a willingness to be responsive both consciously and unconsciously, then we can receive much. Because the transforming power of scripture is healing, helpful, and informational, we are now given one more reason to experience the language of the Bible in this way. The scriptures gently invite us, as readers, into a particular way of thinking, feeling, anticipating, and understanding the text and the world around us. When we seriously consider the aliveness of the biblical words, we are invited into a relationship with the Holy Spirit that changes the way we think, feel, believe, and respond.

To say this in another way, we could look at the world of chemistry and biology. Ernest Rossi has spent much time and energy compiling documentation that hypnotic interactions literally change individuals. Rossi is one of the foremost authorities on trance and using hypnosis for change. His books and lectures are respected around the world in the communities of chemists, psychotherapists, hypnotherapists, and biologists. Rossi's work spells out in detail how interactions and thoughts are conveyed in the body by chemical reactions. These chemical reactions invite molecular changes in a person's messenger cells. As a result of the changes in relating and thinking, the body creates different cells at the foundational, building-block level. When we go into a trance by allowing scriptures to guide us, we are also letting our body, and our mind, to be stimulated by the trance experience. When this occurs, we begin to be recreated in new ways directed by the experience of the trance. Romans 12:2 reads, "Do not be conformed to this world, but be transformed by the renewal of your mind that you may prove what is the will of God what is good and acceptable and perfect." Rossi's work is so important and complete in its treatment of the mind-body connections that I cannot begin to state my appreciation and respect for him. As a result, I will make only this brief reference while extending a serious invitation to readers to follow up by reading Rossi's work for his complete treatment of the biochemical and psychological perspective.

To read scriptures from the non-trance, cognitive perspective, we, as readers, force our own worldview onto the text. When we deny any and all aspects that differ from our own cherished, intellectual interpretations, we are unable to experience the aliveness of the biblical language. While the text might occasionally break through the rigidness of our worldview, it is less likely to happen in a non-trance state.

We can experience an entirely different interaction with the text when we become willing to feel the relational aspects of a passage. One way to encourage such a trance is by treating the scriptures as sacred. The early Hebrews invited a mystical, trance-like experience of the text by using this method. When we image holding "the actual words of GOD" in our hands, we can almost begin to feel this sacredness with reverence and attribute to it the answers to life's problems. Even as we pick up the text, we are already in an altered state of consciousness, because we are anticipating the sacredness of the words. We expect the encounter to have an impact on us, and so we are savoring it. As we touch the scriptures, we are aware of all our senses and we feel close to God.

Once we have received comfort and nurture from a trance state, simply reading and remembering our experience with the scriptures will encourage a similar type of interaction that begins from a particular emotional place locked within us. For instance, hearing a favorite song from a teenage romance 20 years ago can bring back some of the nostalgia of the past. It also raises some of the emotions connected with a particular piece of music and evokes the trance state of the remembered encounter. Allowing the text to hold certain sacredness invokes a similar response because our reverence allows us to appreciate the power of the past engagement as a beginning place while encouraging further movement in the same direction. Many people down through the ages have allowed the scriptures to have an impact on their lives in such a profound way that they changed completely and dramatically. Some attribute physical healing, emotional growth, and recovery of every sort to their connection with scripture. Individuals who chose to believe in the sacredness of scriptures as the text being alive were right. They realized there were ways they could receive the blessings, comfort, information, healing, and guidance that they wanted from scripture.

The whole idea of prayer through the eyes of the Deuteronomic school was to emphasize the importance of recollecting God's mighty acts. They believed that their memory would prompt proper prayer. Even Moses' prayers began with remembrances. By starting with our memories, we set the stage for beginning at the emotional place that we most recently experienced. We in effect become prepared emotionally to enhance today's prayer. This is an effective use of memory and of ritual. Both help to evoke the same type of re-creation we want to reach in the present. If one of our goals is to be in a relationship with God, then this is a helpful avenue to take. However, when prayer becomes a means to manipulate God, then this method will not work any better than any other method, and perhaps even less.

Of course not all people encountering scripture seem to have a conceivable change occur. In fact, through the years many people have become even more stubborn, narrow-minded, harsh, hurtful, and cruel because of their interpretation of the scriptures. Such individuals were sure they had "righteously" understood passages. What most likely takes place is a reaffirmation of secret beliefs. When a person reads scriptures from only one perspective and wants to find that same viewpoint in the written words, they can. As a result, the trance state does not occur since the individual denies any and all aspects of the scripture that disavow their cherished worldview.

If we are willing, the text can come alive and can inform us. Allowing a hypnotic trance of reverence can enhance the sacredness of scripture. It is our anticipation and willingness to encounter a deep experience that makes this possible. Scripture, like any invitation to trance, is only a proposal and will occur only if we are willing to receive from the text. Of course this requires the humility that Proverbs so often refers to as being a part of faith.

Experiencing scripture in this way has given me an opportunity to encounter God at any time. All that is required from me is a willingness to enter the focused attention of the trance while being open to receive from God through the scriptures. This knowledge alone has revolutionized my life. Not only does it mean that I always feel capable of reaching out to God, but I am also given a valuable resource that I can share with others. When I first allow that focused attention to develop within me, then it becomes easier to guide others to a place of peace. When one person is already in a state of focused attention on spiritual things, it becomes easier for others to enter into a similar state. This is an exercise that I intentionally practice before preaching, praying, and counseling.

Before realizing this approach, I never fully understood the reason why people would ask me or someone else to pray for them. It seemed insulting to them. How could one individual's prayer be so much more effective than another's could? Besides, to participate in that type of agreement meant that I was willing to presume that somehow my prayers were superior. I never understood or felt comfortable with what I perceived as an implied insult to a person I cared enough about to include in my prayer. When I consider this in terms of trance, my perception changes. I can gladly be willing to enter into a trance of being aware of God's presence. In this way, I can guide, invite, and encourage a person that I like and care about to be at the place where I am. To pray in this manner seems respectful and appropriate. That implies that the pain, loss, or fear has distracted the person we are praying with from using their ability to pray. If we pray and help, then the person can more easily receive the comforting he or she needs. I welcome the opportunity to assist others in regaining or learning how to receive comfort from prayer. Too often prayer has become an activity or a wish list rather than a real source of comfort and guidance. I believe that this is in part because of our cultural attitude about prayer. When the sacredness of prayer and scripture are gone, where can the sacredness come from? It is only by preserving some aspect of prayer as special, that we set it aside to be sacred. The same is true for scripture. It is only when we set aside the text in order to receive from it that we also allow ourselves to receive.

There are other implications to recognizing the hypnotic nature of the Bible. When we read scripture with an open mind, we are more likely to have the words impact our attitudes, thinking and feelings, primarily through the indirect means that were discussed in earlier sections. Reading the scriptures tends to produce a mindset that is either receptive to the positive implications or one that invokes shame and criticism. Obviously, everyone who reads the Bible does not receive only positive implications. Scriptures, similar to almost every other encounter in life, reflect back mostly what we bring to them. If a person goes to the scriptures feeling shameful, it is especially possible for that person to read the words and quit when he/she feels shamed, criticized, or condemned. It is also possible for a person to read long enough that they come away with a sense of acceptance. Since most of the scriptures' implied messages are below the conscious stated messages, they will probably have more of an effect than the direct messages. This explains why surface ideas found in scripture occasionally do not have as much power to help or comfort a person in crisis. The power of scripture is found in the implied meaning that is received over time. Trance logic is not the normal way we think every day. During a trance, person has a tendency to respond to the hypnotist in childlike, simple and literal ways. This is a typical unconscious form of response and as such, it is a good indicator that a deep trance condition has been established.

Trance awareness is different than ordinary awareness because it affects not only how a person thinks but also on what, and how long. Unlike ordinary awareness, which involves a constantly changing focus of attention, the hypnotic condition involves a focusing of attention and an elimination of distractions. It is not a donation of oblivion, or cognitive unresponsiveness, such as sleep, but a state of consciousness where in the normal hyperactivity of awareness has been reduced and attention has been directed toward a selected set or category of stimuli.

Imagine sunlight as being a normal mindset focused on an idea and hypnosis as a magnifying glass focusing the sun's rays on a particular spot without being scattered. During any waking moment, we screen out sensory data to get through our daily tasks. Right now, we are most likely ignoring the sensations that our feet are also giving us. We can become aware of the sensations of our socks, shoes, and even our bare feet. We screen out sensory material all the time. If we let ourselves become aware of our body and its movements in a more intentional way, we can recognize that we were in an altered state of consciousness. We can recognize that people ordinarily do not pay attention to their bodies and all of the minute movements. Unless we are in a guided trance, we probably will allow something to distract our conscious mind and consequently be off on a tangent to this sensory information and thinking about the application, the pleasure, and the last time you felt really good.... Similar to this last sentence, our attention wanders when we weave in a regular state of mind. It is only in a state of focused attention that people can put deep attention to every movement of their body.

Reading scripture is also going to invite a positive mindset since the implications are positive and indirectly uplifting. Furthermore, the directives and the praising of God indirectly can work toward producing positive feelings as well. If we receive a more positive attitude, it will certainly evoke different chemical and biochemical reactions than if we felt sad, fearful, or angry. If this is true that the reading of scripture produces a certain calm self-assurance, and we can assume that trances impact the body as well as the mind. A number of researchers have identified emotions and thoughts in the body as being converted and carried as chemical messages throughout the body. Thus, the body physically reacts to emotions and thoughts. Psychologists have long-recognized the effects of words on the body. Cognitive therapy has held the position that rather than an actual event it is a person's thoughts about an event that produce the stress for an individual. In other words, stress is produced not by certain situations a person encounters but by the things that a person tells him/herself about the experiences.

So if we read scripture with a sense that the passages will be affirming to us and our goals, life, and health, then the effect will be a positive one for us. Since reading the Bible as a family is often viewed as a positive a way to increase wisdom, the event could easily be paired with warm memories. Reading scripture can also greatly reduce stress and affirm us as whole people. If we are willing to consider that our bodies are an enclosed system with all of its parts impacting our health, then we know that any benefit to us will also benefit our immune system and all systems of our body. Research about emotions and the therapeutic effects of hypnotic interventions gives evidence of this type of impact on the entire system.

Let's look at the reverse side by imagining a person reading scripture who is not at peace with him/herself. While reading the passages, this individual feels, sees, or senses their sin. The feelings of discomfort that the person experiences are something that he/she might be aware of while reading. Continued reading will most likely result in one of three options. 1) The person continues with the inner struggle and attempts to reconcile the behavior with rationalizations. 2) The person chooses to use some form of denial, or the person decides to repent. When the person denies the irregularity of "the sin," and therefore the problem, the positive effect from scriptures is limited. This is because a part of us always knows when we lie to ourselves, even when we are in denial. 3) The individual recognizes the incompatibility and takes steps to repair, by pledging change, or seeking help by turning their behavior and urges over to God, and learning from those occasions if the urge continues. Of course, variations of these three are numerous, and would include actions such as using drugs, engaging in more sin to blot out past sin, overcompensation, and other types of defense mechanisms.

Erickson and Rossi define the therapeutic trance in a way that implies how the reading of scripture is both helpful and potentially healing. This is because a person's unconscious can use scripture in beneficial ways. "Therapeutic trance is a period during which the limitations of our usual frame of reference and beliefs are temporally altered so that we can be receptive to other patterns of association and modes of mental functioning that are conducive to problem-solving."

Almost everyone who has read scripture has had the experience of suddenly seeing a new idea, concept, or meaning that they were not aware of before. I believe that part of how scripture impacts us as readers is through this new perspective, or frame of reference, that we gain.

Reading scripture impacts the mind, body, and spirit. Since what we bring to our encounters can greatly restrict what we receive, all of us will not be positively impacted by scripture. When we bring cynicism, contempt, indifference, or a judgmental attitude to scripture, we are more likely to elicit similar effect within ourselves as we read the scriptures. It follows that when we expect to have a negative experience, then we are likely to receive that as well.

Can reading scripture put us into a trance? No. Can reading scripture invite us into a trance? Yes. Can we go into a positive trance state reading scripture? Yes, if we choose to, because it is our decision first and foremost. If we read the scriptures with an expectation of a response from them to questions held deeply in our mind, then our experience can be a meditative one. Can there still be a question about whether the scriptures are hypnotic or not? Yes, because the bigger question lies in how we define meditation, hypnosis, or trance. There are strict definitions of trance that would not refer to the scriptures as hypnotic. This is due to the fact that they were not defined as hypnotic or because hypnosis was not the intent of the original writers. The difference is how we define hypnosis, hypnotic behaviors, and trance. Regardless of how trance behaviors are defined, the Bible contains the hypnotic devices that have been illustrated.

If we allow ourselves to experience the positive trance that we can receive from reading scripture it can have an impact on our whole mind, body, and spirit. Certainly the relaxation and the calming effect of scripture are almost legendary, yet beyond the calm, beyond the instruction and cognitive information, history, wisdom, "and social learnings, and practical helps, there is a little something extra for your unconscious. Partially that extra is the implied messages that contribute to a sense of wellbeing for believers. Furthermore, if we really have faith in the unconscious, having a positive trance experience with scripture would also be used by your unconscious to rearrange and to alter your life experiences to become more in keeping with behaviors that bring healing, health, and a positive attitude. Another way of saying the above might be this: If you really believe in the Holy Spirit and the way the Holy Spirit impacts your whole awareness, then reading scripture would bring healing, health, and a positive attitude.

Since the scriptures are directly and indirectly concerned with reporting spiritual encounters, we, as readers, also become focused directly and indirectly on our own spiritual dimension. We are invited to have an ideodynamic experience of the spiritual phenomena. For example, when someone in the scriptures is forgiven, we are more likely to experience forgiveness or at least the hope of being forgiven. While in a trance state, a person is usually searching internally for meaning contained in the words. Openness to these internal searches assists us in making the connections between the scriptures and our life.

If we posit that we have a conscious and an unconscious mind, then we can conclude some things about what happens in our mind. Erickson said that the unconscious mind "…does not filter or distort material to suit its perspective or framework because it does not have one." The unconscious mind "…simply perceives, processes and reacts to whatever is indirect or literal manner."

Therefore, what is fed into our unconscious mind is simply there and is unprocessed, unfiltered, and unexamined. As a result, unconscious material becomes a part of the storehouse of information guiding, shaping, and impacting our future decisions. When positive and predictable messages that provide safety are used as foundational information for future decisions, we benefit both now and later.

Because hypnosis involves a state of higher suggestibility, we are more likely to be led to deeper held ideas and attitudes about scripture when we are in a trance state. Of course we do not automatically follow the suggestions given in scripture or in sermon, because we are not automatons but rather people who incorporate into our mix of thinking a unique way of using information. When we seek solutions for certain "problems" in our life, our unconscious mind and conscious mind will search for the information given in a trance state more practically, because the unconscious mind is more willing to recognize the answer. For instance, let's consider a person who is struggling inside about taking one job over another, or of deciding whether to marry a certain person. During a trance state, this person is more likely to extract the useful information needed to make that decision because the defenses of pride or fear are no longer blocking answers. So hearing a story about how another individual made good decisions, the tranced person is now even more likely to hear how to make a good decision, and then simply make it, perhaps not even realizing how their decision was made. In a trance state, a person is free to concentrate on the decision at hand.

A person is more likely to be searching internally for usefulness of information and to accept implied messages about self in a trance state. In other words, a person is usually so sensitive to implied messages and indirect statements that they are likely to go along with hypnotic suggestions as long as the proposals are congruent with the person's experience, beliefs, and values. A listener in a normal state of attention may be more concerned about language used, distractions from uncomfortable positions, or the story as a form of entertainment. When a trance state is deliberately used, the same story might take on a usefulness that the author did not originally intend or could not have foreseen. In a trance state, a person's unconscious mind is searching and will find answers.

The fact that trance has a positive effect on people in ways that go beyond the conscious mind may imply that the conservative readers of the Bible have reason to proclaim that reading the Bible brings answers to those who search for them. There are direct reasons why those answers are found, but the answers that a person creates through their own sinfulness are not any more sacred. The Bible does not block readers whose negativity is so profound that their answers are self-serving. The Bible does reward people, however, who openly trust and seek God's answer over their own. My premise is that no amount of realization about the linguistic ways the scriptures affect us can ever alter the way the Holy Spirit touches us through the scriptures. I think that the hypnotic linguistic structure merely gives evidence of the wonderful nature of the scriptures that we ordinarily recognize.

In addition to the scriptures, other considerations in ministry that use hypnotic devices include preaching and prayer. If the scriptures contain hypnotic devices, then certainly preaching and prayers employ hypnosis in ways that are even more appropriate and respectful. In part, that is exactly what we do when we imitate the words or styles of speaking in our prayers and sermons. I am convinced that the New Testament writers also adopted this style of writing. A hidden message is revealed when we have a deep desire to communicate an important point and choose to imitate a style of writing. When we love and want to communicate something to another person because we love them, we will say it with love implied in our words. Our true feelings and emotions come through in any form of communication. The more powerful we feel our emotions, the more we will be able to express them.

Good preaching of course also has hypnotic dimensions. The most effective preachers use hypnotic devices that empower their messages. Of course such preachers study preaching and are empowered by God because of their faith, dedication, study, grace, and conviction. My contention is that preachers can become even more powerful, helpful and loyal to the scriptures by studying hypnosis. The same argument can also be made with regard to prayer and ministry in general. Most of us share the experience of being with someone praying and felt his or her connection to God. By simply feeling the connection, we also felt close to God and to others present. There are also cases where we have endured a long and boring prayer that someone performed. They may have been sincere and convinced of their prayer's rightness, and yet they were still irksome because they did not take us, as listeners, into account. Occasionally when we are not feeling close to God or others, we have a tendency to try harder or to ignore the distance and hope for the best. On the other hand, when we are feeling close to God, we are likely to also feel near to others as. It is during these ideal moments of closeness that we become willing to consider others' feelings.

Definitions of Hypnotic Devices

Pacing: Pacing is simply walking beside someone in order to help them feel understood. In practice, it means accentuating similarities that can encourage the other person to feel understood, liked, etc. Pacing can be mirroring some action, stance, or tone to communicate support. People who like each other often do this naturally and without concentrated thought. Intentional pacing is similar to saying, "I like you," by stating these words indirectly. Other examples of things to mirror include voice tone, subject, status, position, importance, style, and tempo.

One of the ways the Bible uses pacing is by openly admitting the mistakes of the patriarchs and celebrities found in the text. The outright blunders of these individuals give all of us the sense that we, too, can be accepted. In comparison with the celebrities of the Bible, our mistakes are not so bad. The adventures and sins of Israel, the patriarchs, and the celebrities pace our experiences of making mistakes.

Implied Meaning: According to some linguistic experts, every message has an implied or ulterior meaning. Some specialists assert that a message exchanged between people also contains a message about their particular relationship. Others emphasize implicit meanings that are inherent in both the type and style of the message. For example, the last two lines above infer that this writer assumes a teaching role with the reader. Much if not all of our language is communicated through context, voice tone, facial expressions, etc. Examining implied messages is simply a way of acknowledging the obvious. Since implicit language is part of our everyday speech, it is easy for us to forget how often we use it.

The implied meaning of a sentence is created by the context, attitude, feeling, relationship, qualitative symbol, content, and described behavior. Inferred messages can be sent or received by using or focusing on any of these parts of communication. The words "I love you," for example, can be understood to have a variety of meanings. This text is often said between partners in a new relationship, or by people who are in the midst of pain. "I love you" also symbolizes both superficiality and strong feelings. When we notice the complexity of indirect communication, it makes sense that understanding implied meanings is an ambiguous task.

The way that we interpret the meaning of an inferred message is largely dependent upon emotions, our experiences, and us. For example, if I have felt loved in the past, then my understanding of "I love you" will most likely be different from that of individuals who have not shared the experience of feeling loved. Each reader attempts to understand scripture through a personal lens that contains all of one's limitations and abilities.

A one-dimensional way of looking at the implied meaning of messages can be observed with the following famous illustration. This example depicts how emphasis and understanding change with the use of the comma. "Woman, without her man, is nothing." In this first instance, the emphasis with the pair of commas implies that woman is nothing without her man. Watch what occurs when the comma is placed differently within the sentence. "Woman, without her, man is nothing." By placing the comma and thus the emphasis differently, the meaning of the text is changed. The sentence now infers that man is nothing with out woman.

How we feel while reading the above example is also an important part of the communication. Our perception is important, regardless of whether or not we like or dislike the above illustration. What we bring to the communication is as significant as the words that are actually being said, since our perceptions can transform the entire meaning of the message.

Rapport Building: Rapport building is any device that builds or maintains connectedness. This mechanism involves liking, noticing similarities, or appreciating certain aspects of another person. Puppies are great rapport builders. Through their actions, puppies can evoke positive feelings in us. Their charm, playfulness, and innocence invite us to desire playing with them. Rapport building is generated by the simple act of liking others since this means that we are looking for ways to emphasize connectedness.

Positive Expectancy: Positive expectancy is truly believing in another person. For instance, when we can grasp this concept we will realize how smart we are. Simple belief "in" implies a certain success or achievement. Knowing that someone believes in us is of such great importance that we are often able to do more simply because of that individual's belief.

Simple Conjunctions: Simple conjunctions connect seemingly unrelated ideas together. Because they are connected together, the ideas take on different meanings. For example, while we are sitting and reading these words, and relaxing more and more, we can continue to relax while we recognize that we understand the meaning of, and use of, simple conjunctions.

Confusion: Confusion as a technique is used to distract the conscious mind in order to facilitate acceptance of directives that are normally rejected. People who are unable to receive direct compliments can benefit from this technique. Confusion helps to increase acceptance of implied compliments for persons with low self-esteem. Information overload that is coupled with a series of interruptions is a particular type of confusion tactic. Within an overloaded string of statements, a compliment is interspersed. Since the person obviously cannot remember all of the information given, his/her tendency to dismiss or discount the compliment is erased. It follows that he/she accepts the compliment about self more easily. Individuals who understand this concept deserve recognition for their hard work.

Seeding: Seeding is the act of introducing an idea before it is used. This is accomplished by first placing the concept in our awareness. It is much like giving a preview of coming attractions without actually stating in the present that they are coming. This mechanism helps in preparing us to accept an idea before it is actually introduced. Seeding involves promoting an idea by outlining the ways that others have appreciated and used the concept. It is similar to asking someone if he/she has ever tried to not think about red monkeys, and then asking again if he/she has been able to keep from seeing, playing with, or moving these red monkeys around. Once a concept has been placed in our consciousness, it becomes difficult to not be aware of it.

Implied Causatives: Implied causatives are linguistic ways of connecting ideas to directives so that they are more easily accepted. An implied causative can be experienced by reading the next sentence. As we read these words and become aware of the pages, we will relax with this style more and more. Another example might be that the more we understand this device, the more we will understand how it is used in commercials in order to promote some product.

Syntactic Ambiguity: Syntactic ambiguity is a confusion technique that employs the overloading of text in a sentence, or using syntactic irregularities in order to create a sense of confusion. A mild example of syntactic ambiguity was shown in the previous sentence. This concept is seen in the Apostle Paul's writing when he attempts to communicate a number of different ideas in one sentence. This overloads us with the disconnected connections between concepts.

Indirect Suggestions: Indirect suggestions are suggestions that are made by implication, presupposition, or through context rather than by direct wording. For example, sometime in the future, perhaps in the next few moments, we might begin to understand and really appreciate how indirect suggestions can be used. Indirect communication and suggestions are used regularly as communication devices in the Bible. Since most of what is written in the Bible was written to other people, our reading of the text is indirect communication.

Direct suggestions: Straightforward commands such as "relax and go deeply in a trance" are direct suggestions that are associated with historic hypnosis. Direct suggestions are also about the commands such as "do this, and do not do that." These authoritative commands do not appeal to everyone. Some individuals have an immediate desire to rebel when they hear these types of commands.

Presupposition: Presupposition is an implied idea that is contingent on some idea that is presented as factual, or already accepted. An example of this idea involves the following statement: When you understand presupposition, you can move to the next definition. In the meantime, do you remember what you were doing, or where you were, when you decided to learn more about hypnosis? Of course I have presumed that you decided to learn more about hypnosis. In doing so, I have used a presupposition.

Double Binds: Double binds are concepts that require either compliance or a sudden break in the relationship or communication. If compliance is resisted, then communication is halted midstream. The following example clarifies this point. Would you like to go into a trance to understand binds, or would you prefer to understand trances while finding yourself in a pleasant trance of concentration, or would you rather simply find yourself understanding binds while recognizing that you have been in a pleasant concentration trance in order to understand them? In this example of a double bind, two choices were given, yet neither involved experiencing a double bind. Regardless of which choice we made, we experienced a double bind restricting our other choice. A simpler example may involve the question, "Would you rather understand double binds without being put in one or by being put in one?"

Reframe: Reframe refers to altering the way we view a subject. Reframing pictures with light or dark wood changes our perspective on the picture. Similarly, the way an idea is presented can alter how it is interpreted. The concept is a simple one. Depending on the way an idea is presented, packaged, or displayed, it can be understood through different means that radically affect how others perceive the idea. This entire book is intended to be a reframe of how hypnosis, the Bible, and ministry can be understood. Parables, for example, ideally reframe our interpretation of an idea by altering our expected notions. This is to encourage us to understand the concept from a different perspective. The parable of the Good Samaritan is this type of reframe for the early Jews to whom Jesus spoke. The Samaritan was not necessarily regarded as good, and yet the parable challenges our understanding of what is good, and of Samaritans.

Bibliography

Arndt, William F., and Ginrich, F. Wilbur. A Greek-English Lexicon of the New Testament and other Early Christian Literature. Chicago: The University of Chicago Press Zondervan, 1957.

Bandler, Richard, and Grinder, John. Frogs into Princes: Neuro-Linguistic Programming. Moab, Utah: Live Real People Press, 1979.

_____. Patterns of the Hypnotic Techniques of Milton H. Erickson, MD. California: Meta Publications, 1975.

Barber, Joseph, ed. Hypnosis and Suggestion in the Treatment of Pain: A Clinical Guide. New York: W.W. Norton, 1996.

Barker, Philip. Using Metaphors in Psychotherapy. New York: Brunner/Mazel, 1985.

Brown, Francis, Driver, S. R., and Briggs, Charles A. A Hebrew and English Lexicon of the Old Testament. Oxford: Claredon Press, 1976.

Buttrick, George Arthur, et al., eds. The Interpreter's Dictionary of the Bible. Volumes 1,2,3,4 and Supplementary Volume. Nashville: Abingdon Press, 1962.

Buttrick, George Arthur, et al., eds. The Interpreter's Bible: A Commentary in 12 Volumes. Nashville: Abingdon Press, 1952.

Cohen, Abraham. Everyman's Talmud: The Major Teachings of the Rabbinic Sages. New York: Schocken Books, 1949 and 1995.

Dolen, Yvonne M. A Path with a Heart: Ericksonian Utilization with Resistant and Chronic Clients. New York: Brunner/Mazel, 1985.

Dossey, Larry. Healing Words: The Power of Prayer and the Practice of Medicine. San Francisco: Harper, 1993.

Durbin, Paul. Human Trinity Hypnotherapy. Michigan: Access Publishing, 1993.

_____. Kissing Frogs: The Practical Uses of Hypnotherapy. Dubuque, Iowa: Kendal Hunt Publishing, 1996.

Edgette, John H., and Edgette, Janet Sasson. The Handbook of Hypnotic Phenomena in Psychotherapy. New York: Brunner/Mazel, 1995.

Erickson, Milton H., and Rossi, Ernest L. Experiencing Hypnosis: Therapeutic Approaches to Altered States. New York: Irvington Publishers, 1981.

_____. Hypnotherapy: An Exploratory Casebook. New York: Irvington Publishers, 1979.

Frankel, Viktor E. Man's Search For Meaning: An Introduction to Logotherapy. Boston: Beacon Press, 1959 and 1962.

Fossum, Merle A., and Mason, Marilyn J. Facing Shame: Families in Recovery. New York: W.W. Norton, 1989.

Gilligan, Stephen G. Therapeutic Trances: The Cooperation Principle in Ericksonian Hypnotherapy. New York: Brunner/Mazel, 1987.

Gordon, David. Therapeutic Metaphors: Helping Others Through The Looking Glass. California: Meta Publications, 1978.

Grinder, John and Bandler, Richard. Trance-Formations: Neuro-Linguistic Programming and the Structure of Hypnosis. Moab, UT: Real People Press, 1981.

Haley, Jay. The Power Tactics of Jesus Christ. Rockville, MD: Triangle Press, 1986.

_____. Uncommon Therapy: A Casebook of an Innovative Psychiatrist's Work in Short Term Therapy. New York: W.W. Norton, 1973.

_____, ed. Advanced Techniques of Hypnosis and Therapy: Selected Papers of Milton H. Erickson MD. Orlando: Grune and Stratton Publishers, 1967.

_____, ed. Conversation with Milton H. Erickson MD, Volumes I, II, III. Rockville, MD: Triangle Press, 1985.

Hanlon, Hudson O., and Hexum, Angela L. (comp). An Uncommon Casebook: The Complete Clinical Work of Milton H. Erickson. New York: W.W. Norton, 1990.

Havens, Ronald A., and Walters, Catherine. Hypnotherapy Scripts: A Neo-Erickson Approach to Persuasive Healing. New York: Brunner/Mazel 1989.

_____. The Wisdom of Milton H. Erickson. New York: Irvington Publishers, 1985.

Heusden, Amy Van, and Eerenbeemt, Elsemarie Van Den. Balance in Motion: Ivan Boszormenyi-Nagy and His Vision of Individual and Family Therapy. New York: Brunner/Mazel, 1987.

Hoorwitz, Aaron Noah. Hypnotic Methods in Non-Hypnotic Therapies. New York: Irvington Publishers, 1989.

Keck, Leander E., et al., eds. The New Interpreter's Bible. Volumes 1,2,3,4,5,7,8,9,12. Nashville: Abingdon Press, 1994.

Kittel, Rudolf, ed. Biblia Hebraica. Stuttgart: Wurttembergische Bibelanstalt, 1973.

Kolatch, Alfred J. The Jewish Book of Why. New York: Jonathan David Publishers, 1981 and 1995.

Langs, Robert. The Therapeutic Interaction; A Synthesis. New York: Jason Arsonson Inc., 1977.

Lankton, Carol H., and Lankton, Stephen R. Tales of Enchantment: Goal Oriented Metaphors for Adults and Children in Therapy. New York: Brunner/Mazel, 1989.

Lankton, Stephen R., ed. Ericksonian Monographs Number 1: Elements and Dimensions of an Ericksonian Approach. New York: Brunner/Mazel, 1985.

_____, ed. Ericksonian Monographs Number 2: Central Themes and Principles of Ericksonian Therapy. New York: Brunner/ Mazel, 1987.

Lankton, Stephen R., and Zeig, Jeffrey K., eds. Ericksonian Monographs Number 3: Treatment of Special Populations with Ericksonian Approaches. New York: Brunner/Mazel, 1988.

_____, eds. Research, Comparisons, and Medical Applications of Ericksonian Techniques. New York: Brunner/Mazel, 1988.

Lentz, John. Effective Handling of Manipulative Persons. Springfield, IL: Charles C. Thomas Publishers, 1989.

Meeks, Wayne, et. al., eds. The HarperCollins Study Bible (New Revised Standard Version). San Francisco: HarperCollins Publishers, 1993.

Morrison, Clinton. An Analytical Concordance to the Revised Standard Version of the New Testament. Philadelphia: Westminster Press, 1979.

Ohanlon, Bill, and Wilk, James. Shifting Contexts: The Generation of Effective Psychotherapy. New York: The Gilford Press, 1987.

Poe, Harry L. The Gospel and Its Meaning: A Theology for Evangelism and Church Growth. Michigan: Zondervan, 1996.

Rhodes, Arnold B. The Mighty Acts of God. Atlanta: John Knox Publishers, 1964.

Rosen, Sidney, ed. My Voice Will Go With You: The Teaching Tales of Milton H. Erickson. New York: W.W. Norton, 1982.

Rossi, Ernest L., ed. The Collected Papers of Milton H. Erickson. Volumes I, II, III, IV. New York: Irvington Publishers, 1980.

Steere, David. Spiritual Presence in Psychotherapy: A Guide for Caregivers. New York: Brunner/Mazel, 1997.

Telushkin, Rabbi Joseph. Jewish Wisdom. Ethical, Spiritual, and Historical Lessons from the Great Works and Thinkers. New York: William Marrow and Company, 1994.

Wallas, Lee. Stories for the Third Ear. New York: W.W. Norton, 1985.

Watzlawick, Paul, Bavelas, Janet, Beavin, and Jackson, Don. Pragmatics of Human Communication: A Study of Interactional Patters, Pathologies, and Paradoxes. New York: W.W. Norton, 1990.

Watzlawick, Paul. Munchhausen's Pigtail or Psychotherapy and "Reality". New York: W.W. Norton, 1990.

Zeig, Jeffrey K. Experiencing Erickson. An Introduction to the Man and His Works. New York: Brunner/Mazel, 1985.

_____, ed. A Teaching Seminar with Milton H. Erickson. New York: Brunner/Mazel, 1980.

_____, ed. Ericksonian Methods: The Essence of the Story. New York: Brunner/Mazel, 1994.

_____, ed. Ericksonian Psychotherapy Volume 1. New York: Brunner/Mazel, 1985.

_____, ed. The Evolution of Psychotherapy: the Second Conference. New York: Brunner/ Mazel, 1985.

Zeig, Jeffrey K., and Gilligan, Stephen G., eds. Brief Therapy Myths, Methods, and Metaphors. New York: Brunner/Mazel, 1990.

_____, eds. Developing Ericksonian Therapy State of the Art. New York: Brunner/Mazel, 1988.

Audio/Video Consulted Sources

Andreas. Eliminating a Compulsion. Presented at the Brief Therapy Conference of the Milton H. Erickson Foundation, San Francisco, CA, 11-15 December 1996. BT96:J241-D13.Videocassette.

Baumann. Hypnotherapy with Children in a Pediatric Practice. Presented at the Third International Congress of the Milton H. Erickson Foundation, Phoenix, AZ, 3-7 December 1986. 3rdIC86:PS317-W21AB. Audio tape.

Combs and Freedman. How Did Erickson Get People To Do Those Things? Utilizing Clients' Response Presented at the Third International Congress of the Milton H. Erickson Foundation, Phoenix, AZ, 3-7 December 1986. 3rdlC86:PS317-SC5. Audio tape.

Dolan. The Legacy of the February Man: Ericksonian Age Regression Techniques. Presented at the Third International Congress of the Milton H. Erickson Foundation, Phoenix, AZ, 3-7 December 1986. 3rdlC86:PS317-W23AB. Audiotape.

Erickson-Elliott, Erickson, Erickson, and Erickson. How Milton H. Erickson Encouraged His Children to Develop Individuality. Presented at the Third International Congress of the Milton H. Erickson Foundation, Phoenix, AZ, 3-7 December 1986. 3rdlC86:PS317-TP11. Audio tape.

Erickson, Erickson, Lankton, and Rossi. Keynote Panel: Erickson's Use of Humor. Presented at the Third International Congress of the Milton H. Erickson Foundation, Phoenix, AZ, 3-7 December 1986. 3rdlC86:PS317-K1. Audio tape.

Gilligan. Love in the Face of Violence: A Self-Relational Approach to Psychotherapy. Presented at the Brief Therapy Conference of the Milton H. Erickson Foundation, San Francisco, CA, 11-15 December 1996. BT96:J241-W84AB. Videocassette.

Gilligan, Lange, and Sherman, Stern. Resistance. Presented at the Third International Congress of the Milton H. Erickson Foundation, Phoenix, AZ, 3-7 December 1986. 3rdlC86:PS317-TP2. Audio tape.

_____. Symptom Phenomena as Trance Phenomena...Presented at the Third International Congress of the Milton H. Erickson Foundation, Phoenix, AZ, 3-7 December 1986. 3rdlC86:PS317-W28AB. Audio tape.

_____. The Courage to Love: A Self-Relations Demonstration. Presented at the Brief Therapy Conference of the Milton H.

Erickson Foundation, San Francisco, CA, 11-15 December 1996. BT96:J241-D15.Videocassette.

Gordon. Therapeutic Metaphor. Presented at the Third International Congress of the Milton H. Erickson Foundation, Phoenix, AZ, 3-7 December 1986. 3rdlC86:PS317-W25AB. Audio tape.

Haley, Rossi, and Zeig. Conversation Hour: About Milton Erickson. Presented at the Evolution of Psychology Conference of the Milton H. Erickson Foundation, Las Vegas, NV, 13-15 December 1995. EVOL95:MH260-CH7.

Lankton. Clinical Use of Trance Phenomena for Therapy and Pain Control. Erickson Selected Seminars/Congress Tapes of the Milton H. Erickson Foundation. One Hour Demo. 1983 Congress: V8186-83B. Videocassette.

_____. Hypnosis in Marriage and Family Therapy. Presented at the Third International Congress of the Milton H. Erickson Foundation, Phoenix, AZ, 3-7 December 1986. 3rdlC86:PS317-W43AB. Audio tape.

_____. Methods of Constructing Sophisticated Metaphors for Specific Outcomes of Affect. Presented at the Third International Congress of the Milton H. Erickson Foundation, Phoenix, AZ, 3-7 December 1986. 3rdlC86:PS317-W4AB. Audio tape.

O'Hanlon. Directive Couples Counseling. Presented at the Third International Congress of the Milton H. Erickson Foundation, Phoenix, AZ, 3-7 December 1986. 3rdlC86:PS317-W7AB. Audio tape.

Polster and Zeig. Heroism. Presented at the Evolution of Psychology Conference of the Milton H. Erickson Foundation, Las Vegas, NV, 13-15 December 1995. EVOL95:MH260-D11. Audio tape.

Relinger. Indirect Suggestions in the Treatment of Depression. Presented at the Third International Congress of the Milton H. Erickson Foundation, Phoenix, AZ, 3-7 December 1986. 3rdlC86:PS317-SC29. Audio tape.

Rosen. Group Induction. Presented at the Third International Congress of the Milton H. Erickson Foundation, Phoenix, AZ, 3-7 December 1986. 3rdlC86:PS317-GI-3. Audio tape.

_____. Mind Reading. Presented at the Third International Congress of the Milton H. Erickson Foundation, Phoenix, AZ, 3-7 December 1986. 3rdlC86:PS317-W45AB. Audio tape.

Rossi. Creative Life Facilitation with Hypnotherapy. Presented at the Third International Congress of the Milton H. Erickson Foundation, Phoenix, AZ, 3-7 December 1986. 3rdlC86:PS317-W3AB. Audio tape.

_____. Research Frontiers in the Evolution of Psychotherapy. Presented at the Evolution of Psychotherapy Conference of the Milton H. Erickson Foundation, Anaheim, CA, 12-16 December 1990. EVOL90:PC289-W21AB. Audio tape.

Rossman. Listening To Your Symptom. Presented at the Brief Therapy Conference of the Milton H. Erickson Foundation, San Francisco, CA, 11-15 December 1996. BT96:J241-D2. Videocassette.

Shapiro. Trance on Trial: The Legal Implications of Ericksonian Hypnotherapy. Presented at the Third International Congress of the Milton H. Erickson Foundation, Phoenix, AZ, 3-7 December 1986. 3rdlC86:PS317-SC14. Audio tape.

Simpson III. Diagnosing: Reframing to Help Parents Establish a Context for Change. Presented at the Third International Congress of the Milton H. Erickson Foundation, Phoenix, AZ, 3-7 December 1986. 3rdlC86:PS317-SC33. Audio tape.

Thompson. Conversational Induction with Utilization of Spontaneous Trance. Erickson Selected Seminars/Congress Tapes of the Milton H. Erickson Foundation. 1983 Congress:V8186-83F. Videocassette.

Watzlawick. Psychotherapy of "As If". Presented at the Evolution of Psychotherapy Conference of the Milton H. Erickson Foundation, Anaheim, CA, 12-16 December 1990. EVOL90:PC289-W26AB. Audio tape.

Watzlawick and Madanes. The Construction of Therapeutic Realities. Presented at the Evolution of Psychotherapy Conference of the Milton H. Erickson Foundation, Anaheim, CA, 12-16 December 1990. EVOL90:PC289-12. Audio tape.

Weakland and Fisch. Off the Pedestal: Advantages and Limitations in Erickson's Work. Presented at the Third International Congress of the Milton H. Erickson Foundation, Phoenix, AZ, 3-7 December 1986. 3rdlC86:PS317-W50AB. Audio tape.

Wilson. Strategic Interventions in Panic Disorder. Presented at the Third International Congress of the Milton H. Erickson Foundation, Phoenix, AZ, 3-7 December 1986. 3rdlC86:PS317-W26AB. Audio tape.

Yapko. Building Expectancy. Presented at the Fifth International Congress of the Milton H. Erickson Foundation, Phoenix, AZ, 2-6 December 1992. 5thlC92:ME297-4*s. Videocassette.

_____. Ericksonian Approaches in the Treatment of Depression. Presented at the Third International Congress of the Milton H. Erickson Foundation, Phoenix, AZ, 3-7 December 1986. 3rdlC86:PS317-W11AB. Audio tape.

Zeig. Brief Ericksonian Psychotherapy. Presented at the Brief Therapy Conference of the Milton H. Erickson Foundation, San Francisco, CA, 11-15 December 1996. BT96:J241-D1. Videocassette.

_____. Ericksonian Hypnotherapy. Presented at the Third International Congress of the Milton H. Erickson Foundation, Phoenix, AZ, 3-7 December 1986. 3rdlC86:PS317-W30AB. Audio tape.

_____. Fundamentals of Ericksonian Therapy. Presented at the Evolution of Psychotherapy Conference of the Milton H. Erickson Foundation, Anaheim, CA, 12-16 December 1990.EVOL90:PC289-W33AB. Audio tape.

_____. Guiding Associations. Presented at the Evolution of Psychology Conference of the Milton H. Erickson Foundation, Las Vegas, NV, 13-15 December 1995. EVOL95:MH260-CP1. Audio tape.

_____. Symbolic Hypnotherapy. Erickson Selected Seminars/Congress Tapes of the Milton H. Erickson Foundation. 2 hours, 40 minutes. 1978 Symbols:V8184-8A. Videocassette.

_____. The Personal Growth and Development of the Brief Therapist: Developing…Presented at the Brief Therapy Conference of the Milton H. Erickson Foundation, San Francisco, CA, 11-15 December 1996. BT96:J241-W87AB. Videocassette.

Zeig and Masterson. Ericksonian Methods: The Virtues of Our Faults. Presented at the Evolution of Psychotherapy conference of the Milton H. Erickson Foundation, Anaheim, CA, 12-16 December 1990. EVOL90:PC289-11. Audio tape.

About the author

John D. Lentz D.Min. is the Director of the Ericksonian Institute of Jeffersonville, Indiana, where he practices and teaches Hypnosis. He retired from the Kentucky Correctional Institution for Women after serving 22 years as the Chief Chaplain. While he served as a chaplain he also taught clinical aspects of counseling as an Adjunct Professor for 18 years at the Louisville Presbyterian Seminary.

He is also the author of EFFECTIVE HANDLING OF MANIPU-LATIVE PERSONS Pub by C. Charles Thomas, Springfield ILL.

John is a member in good standing or a supervisor in the following organizations.

American Association of Marriage and Family Therapy, AAMFT, The American Society for Clinical Hypnosis, ASCH, The International Society for Clinical Hypnosis, ISCH, and American Association of Pastoral Counselors, and the Mid Kentucky Presbytery.

He has presented at a number of national and international meetings on subjects including the Bible and Hypnosis, Spirituality, Seduction, Grief, as well as more clinical topics as treatment of various abuse issues, as well as Self Care of the Therapist, and Women Who Murder.

John and his wife Debra live in the Log cabin they built with help from friends, and where they raised two children, Seth and Stacey.

0-595-21720-6